Finding Home:

A Sentimental Journey

To Dave

From

Gemma G. Stemley

Thank You for all the
work you have done to help
me market this book
Blessings Always

Gemma Stemley

For information about this title or to order other books
and/or electronic media, contact the publisher:

Gemma G. Stemley
email: Gemmastemley@comcast.net

ISBN
978-0-578-86338-2 (Hardcover)
978-0-578-95369-4 (Paperback)
978-0-578-93842-4 (Ebook)

Printed in the United States of America

Cover and Interior design: Dan & Darlene Swanson
of Van-garde Imagery, Inc. • van-garde.com

Dedication

FIRST TO MY HUSBAND, CALVIN Stemley, whose idea it was to write in these times of a pandemic.

To the Stemley family for their love and encouragement.

To the many young men and women with whom I had the pleasure of sharing the lessons my mother taught me and who made this journey possible.

To my natural sisters Mia Clarke and Janet Rubie - A sounding-board for the ideas which moved this project along.

To Maria Hernandez Mason who has been a bridge through troubled times.

And to those sisters in harmony and solidarity - Kristen Novak, Barbara Gardner, Teresa Hawthorne.

To my editor Deborah Dunton who is forthright enough to guide me through this creative process.

And to the memory of my mentor, the late Dean John Shropshire.

To you all, I dedicate this book.

NOTE TO READER

There are a few significant terms used in this book which may need clarification.

The first term is home. In the book the term is used to describe the place of my birth, where I took my first tentative steps. I also used the term to refer to a distant place that carries a set of emotional weight and consequences. These sentiments convey the notion of how I experience the feeling of being at home among family and friends. The term is sometimes used in the book in its common everyday sense to describe a place of residence within a community.

The term, Homeland, is Trinidad and Tobago, the country where I was born and the only place where I can obtain a birth certificate. Homeland is imbued with a set of cultural mores and customs into which I was socialized.

Adopted homeland refers to the country in which I have taken up residence, and of which I am a citizen and am in possession of a passport.

Colonize refers to the act of occupying a place – the colony, both politically and economically for the purpose of exploitation of its resources, which is carried out by the group of settlers – the colonizers – on behalf of the of their sovereign.

Imperialism is a policy of domination that takes hold of the economic and political affairs of a weaker and lesser developed country. In the book, Britain as the imperialistic power is also referred to as the Crown.

Text-book English refers to a form of communication that does not include words commonly associated with the creole vernacular, but follows the rules of the English syntax.

Table of Contents

Julia

*"You don't have a home until you leave it and then
when you have left it you never can go back."*

~ James Baldwin

MAY 8, 1902

*At 7.50 am., the people of St. Pierre, Martinique were just getting ready
for the day. Martinique is one of the Windward islands and continues
to this day to be an overseas region of France. It was Thursday morning,
in the year of 1902. Men and women on bicycles could be seen making
their way to the sugar cane factory, the main employer. Horse-drawn
carts jostled for space along the narrowly cobblestoned roads. Farmers
were getting ready to lay out fruits and vegetables for sale in the open-air
markets or along the roadside. Fishermen were on their way to the Docks
to unload the catch from the night before.*

*In every kitchen, mothers were bending over kerosene stoves prepar-
ing the first meal of the day. This consisted of freshly brewed local coffee.
In every yard, in front, or at back of a house could be seen recently picked
red coffee beans which were harvested and laid out to dry in the sun.
The coffee trees, from which these were gathered grew for many years in*

the valleys. They were shaded by lofty Immortelle trees. On this morning, cocoa tea was being prepared by grating the dried cocoa pod and collecting the contents. This powder was added to water and allowed to simmer on the stove to a rich brown consistency. A dash of all-spice was further added to the liquid and seeped for half an hour or so. Then there were the fried bakes to go with saltfish Buljol, which was seasoned with tomatoes, onions, hot peppers and coconut oil.

Sulking boys and girls, as they dressed for school, were hastened on by grandmothers. Fathers set out for a day's work, armed with thermos and brown paper bags with their morning meal. Elderly men and women could be seen sitting out in the sun or strolling along the water's edge, as Saint Pierre is a coastal town. Julia was being transported by tramcar back to the capital city of Fort-de-France, after she had spent a night home visiting her family. She worked with a French emigre couple as nanny to their three-year-old. The temperature as usual was in the mid-70s or maybe a little hotter, but nothing to be concerned about.

Suddenly and without any visible signs, the volcano erupted. The eruption of Mount Pele in Martinique continues to baffle volcanologists to this day concerning the lack of warning. The pyroclastic flowed at a rate of two miles a minute destroying the town of 30,000 people killing everyone except two: a convict and a shoemaker. The convict was in a poorly ventilated dungeon-like cell; the shoemaker jumped into the sea.

Julia escaped the eruption, but her immediate family of three brothers and both parents died that day. She was eighteen at the time. The next day, she, a lone orphan was dispatched by the authorities to a boat leaving for Trinidad to work with a family from England, while her employer returned to France. In Trinidad, she spoke a French creole patois in a country that was occupied by Britain, where most spoke English, or a version of it. The family she worked for taught her English, which she found difficult. Over the years she was servant to several other families before *she finally set up a Roti shop in the city of Port of Spain, from which she was able to make a living.*

Julia was my great-grandmother. While growing up I would visit her often. She lived with her daughter, my maternal grandmother, after she stopped working. Often, she talked about the home she had left behind. Especially in the autumn of her years, she habitually spoke about the time of the eruption and the loss of her family and friends. She recalled the period in the early days when she arrived in Trinidad, and of how isolated and lonely she felt, being away from Martinique, her homeland where her parents were buried with the rest of her family.

She talked about the loss of her language and her culture. Then, after about fifty years, when she could afford it, she returned to Martinique for the first time since leaving. The shock and sadness she experienced upon revisiting the place of her birth, affected her so deeply she refused to go back on a second visit. The changes she had witnessed were colossal. Or maybe it was she who had changed. She was not sure. The image of home for her which she harbored in her mind all those years was illusory. A myth. A whole new generation had emerged, with different ideas and values. Saint Pierre was rebuilt. Nothing remained of the old city. Again, she felt isolated and detached. The past that she knew was sequestered out of view from her memory. Her trip had been about reclaiming the feeling of home. But all to no avail. She returned to Trinidad, crestfallen and complaining about how the world had passed her by. She wanted to know where home was for her, an émigré. Was it the 'here', where she now resided and raised a family? Or the 'there', a place of the past that she could not recognize? Could there be two places she could recognize as homeland? Firstly, was home the place where she could obtain a birth certificate, even though she no longer lived there? Secondly, was home the place where she now lived and was able to obtain a marriage license?

Julia died at the age of eighty. I have kept her experience constantly before me for many years now, especially during the times when I travel from the 'here', to the 'there', and everywhere else, with the hope that I can understand her inquiry of what and where is home for the emigre. Is it the place where my umbilical cord is buried? Or is it the place where I now reside; where I enjoy a community of friends, and where my work with young people is so fulfilling? Can there be more than one place to call home where I can lay my head in comfort and safety?

CHAPTER I

Welcome to the Big Apple

"I went to New York to be born again."

— Kurt Vonnegut

THIRTY-TWO YEARS AGO, MY FIRST entry into my newly acquired passport was stamped - July 14, 1988. I was leaving home for the first time. I felt that the time was ripe for a new adventure. Deciding whether to pursue studies either in Jamaica or the US, I chose the US, since Jamaica was so similar in manners and customs to that of my home in Trinidad. I yearned for a new experience. I like to think of my passport as a kind of journal. Episodic, it is a silent, unwritten story with each date representing a fragment of a personal narrative of arrival and departure. Upon leaving home, this would be a maiden voyage, taking place in the wee hours of the morning. I boarded a red-eye flight to New York, arriving at dawn.

I have yet to witness a sunrise such as the one that welcomed me that morning. The rays of the sun penetrating through the clouds created a landscape that was surreal, and alien. Orange, magenta, green, blue, black, white; the colors of the rainbow welcomed me. It appeared as a tableau painted by an impatient artist to represent chaos, foreshadowing what would transpire as I set foot on foreign soil. I

1

planned to stay one night at a hotel before moving onto campus, so I boarded a taxi and gave him the address.

"Lady there is no Holiday Inn at this address."
"I just made the reservation a week ago." I replied.
"Well, I could take you over there. I think there is a Comfort Inn in the area."

Twenty minutes later he and I approached the check-in counter to determine if I had a reservation or not. I carried my pocketbook, but my luggage was still in the car since I was not sure as to whether this was my hotel. The clerk acknowledged that there was a reservation for me, and that the hotel had changed ownership. The driver and I then got into an argument about the fare. Feeling that the fare was excessive, I paid him what I was told was the going rate for a twenty-minute ride. The driver then stomped off in anger. I assumed he would return with my luggage. Unfortunately, he sped off before I could stop him. The clerk tried to assure me that once he realized he still had the bag he would return it. In the meantime, I was advised to make a police report.

The cop arrived, half an hour later. Tall, white, fortyish. He took my statement and suggested we drive back to the airport to see, if by chance he had returned. No such luck. There was always a slim chance that he would bring the bag to the hotel, the cop assured me. Driving back to the hotel, he wanted to know where I was born and if I was married. He thought I was beautiful and that I must have many admirers back home.

"You look like that girl who won Miss Universe, Janelle something. What was her name again?"
"Oh, you mean Janelle Penny Commissiong."

"Yeah! Yeah!"

"Thank you."

"You here on a visit?"

"No, I'm here to do a Masters' degree."

"Nice! I have to get down to Trinidad for the Carnival. I hear the people from the islands are very friendly," he added.

We were now back at the hotel.

"Thank you. I hope I can get my bag before I leave the hotel."

"My pleasure, hey, mind if I stop by after my shift?"

"I'll be ok." I replied.

He called the hotel later to see if my bag had returned. It had not. He also wanted to know if I was hungry. I was not.

I have often reflected on that first encounter in the Big Apple. I wondered about the name, the "Big Apple." I had heard a story that the name was coined by a woman named Eve who owned a brothel. I was reminded of that proverbial fruit, symbolic of the amoral predisposition of women in the Bible. I thought of the subliminal power of symbols and imagery in everyday life and how it can be mind-altering to the extent that it can influence behavior and ways of thinking. Stereotypes are created in this way.

While living in Trinidad, my perception of New York and New Yorkers had always been, and up to the time of my arrival, of a city that was large and dangerous but at the same time, contemporary and on the cutting edge of technology. I thought of New York as a place whose inhabitants sought release in sensuality and transcendental mysticism as a means of realignment to the soul. This impression was derived over the years from mass media: movies, TV, newspapers, and the tabloids. I had hoped for a positive welcoming experience upon arrival, as a way of softening that image. But this first encounter, upon my arrival, only served to fortify my earlier perceptions. Ironically, I too was being judged by the cop, because of pictures of the islands and the representation of Caribbean peoples he had most likely seen in the tourist brochures. He imagined the Caribbean to be a haven, a paradise in which women were open and welcoming, sensual, and easy to please. He obviously had bought into the stereotype.

Once settled in my room, I witnessed snow falling for the first time. I was looking through the window of my hotel room when it started. It was beautiful. I was amazed at how rapidly it accumulated. It covered any and everything - rooftops, windowsills, cars, trees, fences, and people. The ploughs were working frantically. They backed it into cul-de-sacs, piled it high on mounds, moved it against retaining walls, wherever they could find space. They tried to sequester it out of view behind tall hedges. Snow was everywhere. The winter landscape was so unlike the lush verdant palette of the tropical garden I was familiar with. Winter had painted a garden of a different nature, with trees as stark and bare so that from where I was standing, I could make out every feature of the landscape, every ridge and hollow, the starkness laying bare the trees, branches, and twigs. This frozen world was not totally white but had a palette of pale greens and blues and greys. As I stood there taking it all in from the 6th floor of the hotel room, I forgot about the lost luggage and the brazen cop. My thoughts were of the primordial, of innocence and purity, of a serene landscape devoid of evil, before the Fall. Why the Big Apple, I wondered? This place was no Eden. I could sense a serpentine presence all around. Beneath this snowy blanket of innocence there lurked an unmistakable force that felt ominous.

If ever there was a test of endurance for me, this was it. I began to question whether I had made the right decision coming to this place, which seemed larger than life. I asked myself if I had the grit and determination to survive the Big Apple. Within an hour of arriving, I had lost my luggage mainly clothes and had been hit on by a cop. Depressed and panicky, I called my youngest sister, my fortress and confidante. Always ready to come to my rescue, she had contacted a friend in Queens and suggested that he should stop by to check on me. I was so relieved that I was able to go out and pick up some clothing to replace what was in the lost luggage. The next morning, with a sigh of relief, I boarded a flight out of New York.

CHAPTER 2

The Journey Begins

"How anxiously I yearned for those I had forsaken."

- Fodor Dostoyevsky

THIRTY-THOUSAND FEET IN THE AIR, I reflected on my departure from Trinidad. I thought of my great-grandmother, Julia, who many years ago had to leave the island where she was born to make a better life for herself. The eruption of Mt. Pele in Martinique was the occasion which precipitated her migration to Trinidad. She could not afford the return journey until she was of an advanced age. Now I was embarking on a journey to further my education, but unlike her, for me, the road was clear to return at the end of my program. With her in mind, I thought of the meaning of home.

While living on the island, I felt I knew the meaning of home and homeland. Home was invested with feelings for family, friends, traditions, and a place where I would always be welcomed. Homeland on the other hand was the country where I was born and the only place where I could obtain a birth certificate. It was also where I first learned a language and culture that identify me as a woman of Trinidad. I wondered if I could experience the feeling of home elsewhere. Can it be shared? Can the idea of homeland be associated with other categories besides birthright? When one becomes a naturalized citizen of a country, does that country become homeland as well? Furthermore, can homeland be shared? Those early days working on my degree was also a time when I thought constantly of my life in Trinidad and how it contributed to my notion of home.

I grew up poor. My two sisters and I shared hand-me-downs. In spite of our poverty, my mother always encouraged us to set our sights upwards and outwards, beyond our village where there was no chance of improvement. She was adamant that we should not become too comfortable in the village. For to remain in the place where we grew up would be to continue the cycle of poverty. She instilled in us the notion that we needed to pursue and make full use of education because it was the only way out. There would be no inheritance. All that we possessed was our brain, and we should "make use of it."

I took to heart this sound advice. I was on a journey for self-improvement. Where would this odyssey take me? While in flight from Trinidad to New York, I recall I did not experience any feelings of anxiety or of dislocation. In fact, the journey was so commonplace that had I not been in the air, it could have been just another bus trip to Port of Spain. Being in the cabin, for all intents and purposes, I felt as though I was still in Trinidad. Everyone on the plane spoke the same language, sharing jokes about the political intrigue that was rife on the island. From time to time, we even broke out into song. We were served a local meal and could order local drinks. The Trinidad rum Old Oak was available for purchase. We spoke to one another as though we had been all from one big family. And we were. We were all Trinidadians travelling together. We shared the same culture, one in which we were at ease with one another.

Later that day, everything changed when I boarded a connecting flight to Pittsburgh. I immediately felt the distance. I was no longer in my "Trinidad-ness". The familiarity and comfort had vanished. It no longer felt like home. I was out in the cold without the comfort of the blanket which was home to me. I could not help but notice that all around me people moved about with such determination and confidence. I, on the other hand, felt lost and displaced.

During the flight, there was such a deafening silence among the passengers, quite unlike my journey from Trinidad to New York, that I yearned for companionship. I must have stood out in contrast to all the passengers on the plane. I wondered what they thought of me. Once in a while, the bits and pieces of conversation that reached my ear were completely foreign to me. The language was the same, but the accent was different. It was not unpleasant. In fact, it gave the impression of calm assurance, unlike the short, punctuated impatient way we Trinidadians spoke to one another. I was filled with misgivings. Perhaps I should have chosen to do my studies in Jamaica where all things were familiar. Maybe I was too hasty in deciding to come to the US, but the dice was cast. There was no turning back.

Among the lessons my mother taught us her daughters was one which advised that the best course of action was to build a solid foundation, preferably before marriage. My mother talked constantly of not being able to escape the ravages of a meagre existence due to a lack of education and opportunity. She always wanted more for us. These sentiments became so ingrained in us, her daughters, that they were worn as a kind of second skin. Sheltered by my mother's hopes and dreams for me, I took my first job as a Library Assistant in the public library after graduating high school. I was always a big reader and felt the library would be a place I could build a career and find inspiration. Some years later, I moved to the University of the West Indies Library, with better pay and health benefits.

I was eighteen when I met my first husband. He was the older brother of one of my friends. He had been a widower with a young son. We lived together for almost three years before deciding on marriage. My husband belonged to one of the minority groupings in Trinidad having Portuguese ancestry, commonly referred to as Trinidad white. He was much older than I by several years. His mind was set on farming. Soon after we were married, he chose to lease a small farm with a few animals. His idea was to take early retirement and to pursue farming on a larger scale. At the time of our marriage, he worked as a clerk earning good money and benefits. He could supplement his income with the proceeds of the farm.

At first, I continued working after we were married but then I decided to leave the job to pursue further studies at the University of the West Indies. My plan was to take up studies in the Social Sciences, in Economics and Accounting. Instead, I enrolled in a degree program in Agricultural Sciences on the advice of my husband, who felt it would be useful later if we were to take up farming in a big way. It soon proved to be an ill-advised move. Staggering under the heavy load of the natural sciences - Chemistry, Biology, Zoology, labs, and more labs, I barely survived my freshman year. Finally, my determination and resilience grounded to an abrupt halt.

I realized from an early stage in my life that I had a tendency to shrink away from expressing my true desires and needs. I frequently found myself acquiescing to others' suggestions and ideas, thereby rejecting my own aspirations and plans. I found this to be true especially where men were concerned. I saw my reluctance to speak up for myself as an example of a sort of unconscious acceptance of male dominance. This was an idea so entrenched into my psyche that capitulation seemed natural. Furthermore, instead of experiencing my compliance as being an admirable quality which could lead to altruism and modesty, it was often debilitating and counterproductive to my goals.

As I reflected on the impact of my first marriage on my career plans, several thoughts occurred to me. One thought was that books on relationship-building in marriage always stress the need for compromise, of sometimes having to lay aside one's desires and hopes to satisfy the wishes and aspirations of one's spouse. But what is not often revealed is the aspect of oneself that should be surrendered and those that are worth cherishing and preserving. In my case, the idea of the farm was not what I wanted, but I agreed to go ahead with it because of him. I had relegated my hopes and dreams for those of my husband's. Perhaps if I had, from the beginning, articulated what my aspirations were instead of going along with my husband's plans, I would have fared better. But I was hampered by a lack of courage. Later, I came to a better understanding of compromise, of give and take. In any marriage, there is a pursuit that continues throughout the life of the relationship, and I imagine with the right person it could be an adventure. Hence the search is always to find the mate with whom one shares many things in common, thereby reducing the stress to strike a happy balance. So, armed with my new confidence in expressing what my desires were, a few years later, I announced that I wanted to get back on track with my plans to return to my studies. This did not bode well for the relationship and it marked the beginning of the end.

Reaching back to my original interest and plans, I decided on a degree in the Social Sciences which was better suited to my interest. My obtaining a bachelor's degree in Economics and minor in Accounting allowed me to return to the library. My husband's hope was that still

I would be a stay-at-home wife and farmer. When I graduated with my bachelor's degree and then mentioned my interest in doing a master's he became increasingly disturbed and unhappy. Furthermore, I explained that it would have to be in Jamaica or America, since a program in Library Science was not offered in Trinidad.

I wondered, what is this fire in my belly? Why this thirst, this urge to make something of myself and to break the cycle of poverty? What is its source, its wellspring? From whence arose its authority? Is it the memory of childhood growing up in an environment surrounded by despair, deprivation, and the consequent lack of opportunity for my parents? My mother lived vicariously through us her daughters. In some mysterious way her aspirations for us, for me, filtered through my everyday decisions and gained primacy. I knew I should be self-reliant, and able to support myself. Most importantly I knew I could not be held back by anyone from developing my full potential and arriving at the essence of who I was.

I felt that leaving Trinidad would mark the onset of new beginnings for me. I knew that leaving the life of the past may entail venturing beyond what was familiar. I had plans to return but not necessarily to my husband. Although I was about to chase after my dreams, I looked forward in anticipation to a day when I could return to the land of my birth. For home was where I belonged and where I took those early tentative steps. While I was leaving home for a short time, it would feel better when I returned. I would be welcomed with open arms back into the Trinidad and Tobago -Trinbago family where I could feel secure. For this was what home meant to me when I left to pursue my studies. Unlike my great-grandmother Julia, I had no reservations about its meaning, when I first left. It was a place imbued with the memories of growing up and where I could go to find shelter during the storms of life.

CHAPTER 3

Making Adjustments

"You can live here all your life, and still be considered an outsider."

- E.D. Rea

THE NEXT STOP ON MY journey was a college in Western Pennsylvania on a predominantly white campus in a small town with a ubiquitous Main Street. Arrangements were made through the International Student Office for me to rent a trailer not too far from the campus. It was owned by two women in their mid-sixties. They were very gracious to me during the time I was a tenant. They referred to me always as the – "colored girl" not the woman of color, or the Black woman. Strangely, I have never seen "colored" as a designation of race and ethnicity whenever I fill out forms in the US. It was my first encounter in the United States with people who live below the poverty line. Unwittingly, I became a member of a trailer park community.

That first winter, I developed a curious way of walking as if I were treading on eggshells. While everyone around me seemed comfortable hustling from one place to another, I inched along slipping and sliding. I felt embarrassed whenever I saw children playing in the snow. Their incredible adaptability in freezing temperatures, tunneling through mounds of snow, in their make belief world of igloos and caves was, frankly, amazing. I was envious of their casual indifference to the cold and ice. Someone suggested I should buy shoes with ridges on the bottom. That did not help much either.

During those early days I was not my usual effervescent self. I forced myself to think of creative ways to be transported out of the abysmal cold and freezing temperature. I found some comfort in the one thing that had gained primacy in my mind ever since my arrival. I thought of home. Constantly. I was concerned about my mother who was struggling with depression. I wanted her to know I was moving "outward and upward" just as she had advised and hoped. Several months before I left Trinidad, she had been so ill that as a result, she hardly knew who I was by the time I left for the United States. My father had retired and was still in fair health.

On those occasions when I thought of home, I was often reminded of the hot midday sun. I imagined myself on the beach looking out into the placid turquoise water with an occasional break of shimmering highlights of speckled silver. I thought of colors mostly yellow and green. I thought of fruits and flowers. I thought of the Trinidadian artist, M.P. Alladin's paintings of colorful streets and village scenes. His rural settings were folksy and pleasant. I pictured Leroy Clarke's magnificent landscapes and abstract works with its profusion of color, flamboyant and zestful with a deep sensitivity. I thought of my favorite foods. There was no comfort in campus cuisine. I thought of that big creole extravaganza for which Trinidad is famous. There was an alluring vision of myself in my mind's eye of myself in costume as the Queen of the Nile, resplendent on Carnival day.

Whenever I observed the winter landscape, I refused to think of monochromatic still-life scenes. I tried to imagine how an artist in Trinidad would transform the bleakness into vibrancy. I am always surprised to discover that the winter landscape is devoid of fragrance. To me there is a distinct absence of aroma. I wondered how the natives handle this unending coldness, this unvarying monotone. Walking through town, I was baffled about how quiet everything seemed to be. It was as though the townsfolk had receded into a secluded place, to which I did not have access. I often felt that I was required to undergo a sort of rite of passage, or an initiation, before I would be allowed to share the secrets of winter survival.

With arrival to any new country there is a definite period of adjustment. One must first wade through a sea of cultural norms that are uncommon. For me, language posed the first hurdle. I had left an English-speaking country to study in another country where English was the first language. When I decided to study in the US, I did not anticipate problems with communication. I was used to an easy going colloquial, everyday form of expression at home, with words and phrases unique to Trinidadians. Fortunately, I could communicate when it was necessary, in 'text-book' style English.

I soon discovered, however, that my difficulty with communicating was not with the syntax of the language itself but with phonetics. The way I pronounced words was uncommon and foreign to people with whom I interacted. My "twang" confused them. The conversational style I knew and was accustomed to with its rhymical inflections and accentuated phonetic patterns on words and phrases, colored my diction and the way I expressed myself. It was unintelligible to the average person. To further complicate matters, I discovered that many of the people in the area also had a form of dialect that was regional. Often, I too, had difficulty understanding it.

Out of necessity, I had to learn a whole new way of communicating within the language. Delivery was also an issue. In the beginning, on many occasions, I was asked to slow down when speaking 'textbook English.' Slowly, there were modifications, with changes in the way I emphasized words and sounds. For example, I had to be careful about the "th" sound at the beginning of words. 'Textbook English' soon became the language of communication I utilized in the college setting. However, creole dominated those conversations I had with myself. When I wished to castigate, challenge, and up-braid myself for my actions, I employed my inner Creole parlance. I chose Creole because the appropriate word could not be found in the English dictionary. On those occasions when I spoke to myself, I used the form of the Trinbago vernacular, which sounded something like this:

> Ay yai yai! Ah bazodee, yes? - I am so stupid,
> Ah chut! Ay so dotish. - Doltish. For heaven's sake!
> Ay is an imp. - I am dimwitted and dumb.
> Ay tell you. - That I surely am.
> How I so chupid? - How could I be so stupid?
> Ask meh this question. - Ask me that question.
> Ay is a chupidee. - I will tell you, I am foolish.
> Ay is a cunumunu. - I am a fool.

I was constantly being reminded of that objectionable character of the "Freshwater Yankee" who, having been to the US on a short visit goes back home affecting an accent that is American. This artificiality has been a favorite topic for comedy and calypso over the years within the Trinidad culture. The calypso singer, The Mighty Conqueror sang about such people. I was determined not to be one. Some adjustments were necessary, but the nasalized drawl which is unique to Americans in their everyday manner of speaking, does not come naturally to me. I once was asked how I managed to retain such a strong accent after living in the US for so long. My response: why not?

As time went on, I planned to use my experience of working in an academic environment while in Trinidad, to secure student employment at the college. Once the semester began, I applied for, and was granted an assistantship in the Admissions Office. Little did I know at the time that this would prove to be the foundation for establishing a career in college admissions in the years to come. As a graduate assistant I would be working behind-the- scenes writing letters and making cold calls to prospects. Occasionally I would be attending college fairs with a recruiter to target minority students: African American, Latino, Asian American and Native American. I would also be able to visit high schools, most of them in the inner cities throughout Pennsylvania. In those early days, I looked forward to an opportunity to travel in areas beyond the campus where there was a possibility of meeting people from the Caribbean and Trinidad. For me, these encounters often served to keep the memory of home alive.

During those early days while interacting with fellow students and faculty, I discovered they had feelings similar to mine – a developing sense of belonging that conflicted with the yearning to return to the place which they referred to as "home" where they had grown up. I listened to accounts of their childhood experiences and was able to identify with the nostalgia and longing they felt. Whenever I asked them where home was, invariably the answer was associated with either a small town or city. On several occasions I met the children of military families who had been born in one state and grew up in several other places on military bases. In every case, there was a sort of ambivalence about identifying one place as home. There was a tendency to accept that the meaning of home could be applied to more than one place – the town in which they were born, as well as some other place or places where they had spent most of their childhood.

CHAPTER 4

Campus Culture

"Education is the best provision for life's journey."

- Aristotle

THE INTERNATIONAL STUDENT BODY ON this campus was small. Most of the students were from Africa, India, and China. I represented the entire Caribbean region. The office of International Student Affairs is set up to help students to settle on or off campus and to develop programs to ensure that they integrate into American culture. There appeared to be little interaction among the majority students on campus and this group. I was surprised that African American students on campus, being part of a small minority group, did not try to reach out in solidarity.

This cultural divide between international and American students, more specifically black and white students could be attributed to the fact that intercultural pursuit was not a priority. Realistically, foreigners in the US are regarded as the 'Other', not part of the group, the clan, or the citizenry, a transient with an indecipherable accent. Cultural events on campus with food and national costumes and music were always well attended by the rest of the campus community but beyond that, integration was minimal. My program in

Library Science numbering forty students had two minorities, myself, and an African American gentleman. These students were older and hailed from all over the US. Many of them knew something about the Caribbean area. However, their knowledge of the islands ended with Jamaica. Often, I would be questioned about the type of government in Trinidad, the religion, language, food, culture and Janelle Commissiong, Miss Universe from Trinidad and Tobago.

College campuses in small towns provide a unique haven for students with little need to interact with the local townsfolk. My own encounters with the people of the town were sporadic at best. On occasions, when I was out grocery shopping, I would see them, but there was little interaction. The college was the main employer for skilled and unskilled workers. The town-gown relationship was generally cordial. However, the townspeople's primary concern was the weekend parties, and the noise and traffic congestion generated by the students on Main Street.

Apart from the economic benefits to the community, cultural programs were offered but were marked by low attendance or interest from the local residents. On these occasions I generally would see one very elderly gentleman, stooped over and leaning on a cane. Rain or shine, he was always there. I often saw him in the library on campus. I was told he had been an English Literature professor many years ago. I decided to approach him and introduce myself. That marked the beginning of a beautiful friendship. Our first conversation took place in the library and went this way:

"You taught English Lit, I understand?" I queried.

"Yes. You know anything about English Lit?" he inquired.

"I grew up in Trinidad. It used to be a colony. We read Dickens and Hardy in High school, Bronte and Jane Austin."

"I am surprised. You had Naipaul and C. L. R. James and Samuel Selvon then, didn't you"?

"Yes. It's the same old story of a prophet not welcomed in his home-town." I replied.

"What do you think of Conrad's book <u>The Heart of Darkness</u>?"

"Not very much." I responded.

"How so?" His expression one of curiosity

"Like the European of his day, Conrad was sold on the image of the backward childish African. He never investigated into what was going on in those communities." I countered.

"But he was equally negative about his character Kurtz, the white settler whom he portrayed as depraved." He probed.

"Oh no, you don't understand. Childishness is a very disparaging way to refer to a people. But cunning and guild and the ability to hood-wink someone and force them to do your bidding, that is what constitutes progress in his estimation. The mind that can exploit others and whole nations and strip them of their resources - that is advancement."

He smiled and took my hands in both of his. *"I am glad you stopped by to introduce yourself. We have much to talk about."*

"Yes! Let's begin with why you are the only person I see from the town at the cultural events on campus?"

He nodded his head knowingly, sadly explaining, *"Most of the inhabitants are blue color workers. Very conservative."*

I suggested, *"I would think, the college would be a great place for the public at large to keep up with what's going on in the world."*

To further explain he said. *"Habits die hard. Many of these people have never left town and the world is a distant place. The young ones who graduate from here don't stay."*

This was the first of several conversations we enjoyed about literary works written by American, British, and Caribbean authors. We must have presented a charming picture huddled together in the library, in the cafeteria or just sitting around on a nice day talking about life in general. I, a youngish Black woman, and he in the autumn of his years, engaged in deep conversation. He was a fount of knowledge on American History. I appreciated the time he was able to bring me up to speed with the day-to-day happenings on the political scene. He was Canadian by birth and had left to pursue studies in the US many years ago. He ended up staying because of work opportunities and marriage. He had a son who was living in New York. His wife was no longer alive. In a way, we were both foreigners.

In one of our subsequent conversations, I asked. *"Do you consider America or Canada to be your home?"*

He replied, *"Both. I was born in Canada, but my wife was an American. Home can mean many things, not just about natality."*

Looking for clarification I probed him further. *"So, it is possible to find meaning in a place where you were not born and then to consider it as home?"*

"Sure!" he offered. *"Try not to always think of home as place but of relationships and people."*

"How is that possible?" I asked.

"I'll give you an example," he continued. *"I think it was during the time of the Peloponnesian War in Ancient Greece in the fifth century BC, the people of Athens were worried about their homeland being destroyed. The King responded by pointing out that Athens could be created anywhere simply by relocating its people. That a people made a land not vice versa."*

I said, *"I understand. Now I see how folks like Stokely Carmichael and others can adopt a different country as their home. They have found meaning and relevance elsewhere."*

He offered the following examples from his own experience. *"Yes, my folks grew up in Germany. They were Jews and had to flee for their lives under Hitler. That is how they ended up in Canada where I was born."*

I confirmed my own understanding. *"I understand what you are saying. That the winds of change in politics and economics can throw a wrench in the way we define our nationality." "Yes. The Weimar Republic in Germany in 1933 gave way to a totalitarian regime that redefine who should be a citizen. It could happen very easily anywhere if we the electorate are not careful."*

"I am surprised how few Americans don't vote, in particular Black folks. Don't they know their history?"

He clarified: *"They see little difference in either party to improve their condition."*

"Is that what it is?" I asked.

"Maybe so."

With each day, my experience as a graduate international student was becoming less isolating primarily because of my association with the Admissions staff as their Graduate Assistant. The few minority graduate students on campus had assistantships and enjoyed mentoring relationships with Black faculty. Subsequently, we were drafted into a group on campus called the Black Caucus, which was a sister body to a much larger statewide organization comprising of minority staff and professors in higher education. This proved to be beneficial in many ways. It provided a source of knowledge as to how educational institutions operate and the problems minorities experience with achieving tenure track positions. I was able to gain some insight into the barriers in the system that mitigated against the hiring of Black faculty and administrators.

My association with this group was very enlightening. As an international student, I was vaguely concerned with American politics, history, and literature. However, that all change with my membership into the Black Caucus on campus, where I met regularly with Black faculty and administrators. As the Graduate Assistant to the Dean of Admissions who was the leader of the group, I was drafted to serve as the secretary for this organization.

With the acceptance into the Caucus, I felt that I was propelled into an exciting cultural space, a new milieu with a glimpse into the body politic of which I knew little. I was delighted. What euphoria! I had become a member of the clan. I had found a kind of cultural shelter. I seemed to be acquiring a new identity. What was it? Now I was seen as African American. I ceased to hang with the Internationals. With this new acceptance I felt it was incumbent upon me to explore what nationhood was to the African American community. I wanted to learn about the Black experience in America.

I plunged into a full-scale study of black literary works. I read Zora Neal Hurston, James Baldwin, Alice Walker, Toni Morrison. I mourned the obscurity of "_The Invisible Man_" as told by the author Ralph Ellison. Night after night, I perused the literature on inequality and disenfranchisement. I scrutinized articles on the so-called stereotypical disfunction of black families. I bemoaned the plight of inner-city youth and Black on Black crime. I already knew of the horror of slavery. It was a sort of touchtone, informed by a common history and linked to a shared origin on the African continent. Gradually, I perceived that I was moving further away from foreignness and the 'Other'. I was beginning to be assimilated into the subculture of being considered a Black American. This encounter precipitated an unveiling of a new self, a new hybrid identity - with one foot in the Trinidad cultural landscape and another in the Black community.

During these early days, I had little contact with home. Social media was yet to be a reality. The use of the World Wide Web was confined to the developed world. It had only recently arrived in the Caribbean. Cell phones were new, while foreign calls were prohibitively expensive. I had no idea about what was taking place in Trinidad. My communication through snail mail with family and friends was sporadic, eventually petering out to a minimum. Subsequently, this newly acquired acceptance on campus, helped to ease my longing for my family at home. My hybrid identity was one which was characterized by thinking in the Trinidad vernacular, but communicating in 'text-book' English. In time, I slowly learned the latest slang and cool sayings. I also had to develop the habit of always making direct eye contact. I began to dress more casually in muted colors so as not to stand out. I surmised that this was the beginning of a process of acculturation.

Slowly I was beginning to gain some insight into a new way of defining the notion of home. Might it not also include places where self-actualization was possible? In other words, rather than simply be confined to country of origin, might there also be places where one can be of service, feel accepted, welcomed, trusted, supported, and respected? Other than for purely economic or educational reasons, there would of necessity, need to be a compelling reason why the many men and women who have left Trinidad over the years, and have settled in foreign lands came to consider these places as home. I wondered about this transformation.

Did they consider these adopted countries places where they would not be turned away, or where they would be welcomed with opened arms? Was this home a place where they could lay their heads comfortably at night?

CHAPTER 5

Change in Status

"Go confidently in the direction of your dreams!"

-Henry David Thoreau

DURING MY TENURE AS A graduate assistant, I volunteered to write a couple of grant proposals for the Admissions Office that were subsequently funded. The money from these grants provided the resources to bring national speakers such as Julian Bond and Randall Robinson to speak to students, faculty, and townsfolk on campus. I also had some ideas about establishing a mentoring program for minority students on campus, using Black and White faculty. I suggested including upperclassmen/women in the mentoring program to promote retention. Without my being aware of it, I was slowly proving to be an asset to the university. When an opportunity arose to work as a recruiter, I was encouraged by members of the Black Caucus to apply for the position. As a result of my experience up to this point, I discovered something about the American set of values when it comes to 'doing business'. You were respected if you could improve their bottom line.

My first reaction to the prospect of being considered a suitable applicant and possibly getting the job was elation! Shortly thereafter, this feeling of euphoria slowly gave way to one of guilt and disloyalty. I felt tremendously conflicted. How could I even consider taking up employment in a country that was not my homeland? I felt I had a duty to return home and share what I had learned and experienced. What sort of person, I asked myself, chooses to work in a foreign country rather than her own? Such was the height of betrayal, I felt. This self-flagellation went on for several days. I was so consumed by this feeling of disloyalty to my fellow countrymen at home, that I was unable to complete the job application. In Genesis 25, Esau refers to Jacob who 'sells his birthright for a mess of pottage.' I felt that the Prophet was referring to me. That I should even consider such a move, as a means of augmenting my career was difficult for me to justify.

I decided to call home. I was able to get through to my mother on a long-distance call at a time when she was most lucid. I spoke of my dilemma and how I felt about not applying for the position. Her response was unequivocal. "Carajo!" she shouted. "Bull shit! Upward and outward is what I always say. Make use of the opportunity." The very next day I applied for the job.

I was very excited to have landed the position. As my journey continued, it was propelling me further into the body politic. My identity now fell within the ethnic categories set out by the Federal Government. For the first time since arriving, I was required to fill out all types of forms associated with a change in immigration status. On the forms, I checked the box Black/ non-Hispanic, as all other categories were inappropriate. This suited my newfound hybrid identity, enabling me to be identify with both the African American community and the Trinidadian culture.

As a result of my new status, many doors were opened. I was placed on an H1B visa which allowed me to earn a living only with the employer with whom I was contracted. I was able to travel in and out of the US. I could drive and was issued a social security number. I could open a bank account and to my amazement have numerous credit cards. Certain unalienable rights were extended to me, such as the right to be represented by the University's legal counsel. I could own property. Regrettably, I could not take up another job on the side to earn additional part-time wages. I could not vote in any type of Federal or Municipal elections. Filing my tax return in a timely manner was advised.

In the space of a few years, I had been able to complete my master's degree and to gain employment. This meant that I was not on track to return home immediately. It was a clear indication that I was now on course to "achieve the American dream." My paperwork, which was needed to start employment came through at the end of my program. It coincided with the beginning of summer and I decided to move closer to the campus. Despite all of this progress, I still struggled emotionally. As with Esau's condemnation, I felt burdened by the feeling that I was selling my birthright 'for a mess of pottage.' Despite my mother's advice, I continued to struggle with a lingering sense of betrayal. My conflict caused me to second guess my choice to emigrate to the United States. I worried about retribution from a higher authority. Would I be castigated, and then need to seek atonement? I tried to vindicate myself by exploring ways to make up for the betrayal that I carried within me. To that end, I wrote letters to prospective students from Trinidad, who had an interest in the university. On one of my visits to Trinidad, I spoke to high school students about college admissions. Despite these valiant efforts, I seemed to have more luck with the children of Trinidadian parents who had settled in the US. Some of these students were born in Trinidad while others were born in the US.

Once I was settled in my new job, I found an apartment that was recently vacated by a college professor who was moving back to her hometown in Illinois. It was a beautiful, old, wooden colonial house that was once the home of an estate owner. It had been converted into apartments. I felt lucky to have gotten one with a balcony on the second floor. Across the street was a bed and breakfast, another colonial in design. The street was lined with century old weeping willow trees. I moved in over the summer and spent many a night with the adjoining door to the balcony open. Before I knew it, fall turned to winter and I froze, inside and out.

In my haste to move into a bigger place closer to the campus, I neglected to consider any of the practical considerations one makes when renting a new place. I certainly gave no thought to the changing seasons and what that would physically entail. I was none the wiser about heating systems and windows that allowed the cold air in because they needed replacement. I made the decision solely based on cosmetic appearances. I loved the large bay windows that allowed the light in. It provided a perfect home for Boston ferns and hibiscus plants, little tea roses and anthuriums. This colorful, verdant, lush space was soothing and reminded me of my tropical home. Unfortunately, I had signed a lease. I was here to stay.

With blinders on, I sometimes saw "through a glass darkly." The apostle Paul, himself a traveler and foreigner to many different places, coined that phrase. In selecting the apartment, my Caribbean frame of reference was totally unsuited to the new reality of a northeastern climate with four seasons. My ability to adjust and become acclimated to this new home was indeed complicated by my life-long experience living on a tropical island. One which had taken me years to develop from birth to adulthood. It was clear I needed a completely new frame of reference.

Beyond having to acclimate to the weather and the seasons, there was need for adaptation on a more cerebral level. I needed a functional way of interpreting this unfamiliar place. I thought about how I could guard myself against vulnerability and defenselessness and at the same time, adjust to my new reality. I contemplated how I could create a new frame of reference. Does experience naturally lead to a new and perceptive way of knowing? How long will it take to acquire? Maybe it is never totally perfected. I considered how tourists, anxious to escape to a paradise arrive with a frame of reference, and preconceived notions, formed by tourist brochures, promotional videos, and glossy magazines. Typically, tourists have little concern for, or interest in, the authenticity of an island's culture, history, or social and economic issues. Promotional materials designed to encourage tourism are devoid of the realities of people living in a poor third world nation. But those realities most certainly exist. I could not see all the inherent flaws of the apartment because like the tourist, I was blinded by the desire to recreate Eden.

I discovered Philadelphia during my first year of recruitment as an employee. The "City of Brotherly Love" possessed some of the worst projects I'd ever seen. They surrounded the well-established universities as Temple University on Broad Street, the Ivy League University of Pennsylvania, and Drexel University. For me, it was a classic case of deracination of poor communities. These giant institutions expanded in all directions by supplanting poor Black urban populations. Through my work, I discovered that students in the Philadelphia public schools were the least prepared for college entry.

Still, I loved Philadelphia. The diversity was incredible. Whenever I was recruiting in Philly, I often ran into Trinidadians. Then I would relax into the Trinidadian dialect with a sigh of relief. I would get all the latest news and gossip. Who was the Prime Minister? Who won band of the year during the Carnival? Who was the Calypso King? I found out the best places to get a good roti in Philly. There was a large contingent of Caribbean peoples living in Philly. The annual Carnival was as impressive as that of New York or Toronto. It was a smaller version of Trinidad's with calypso, steel band music and masqueraders. I looked forward to my visits to Philly as they offered me a feeling of rejuvenation. At the same time, I experienced a reconnecting with my Trinidadian roots which were ever present in my subconscious mind.

On one such trip to Philadelphia, I recalled a visit to a supermarket in the heart of the Black community on Broad Street. The smell of guavas, as I entered the produce isle brought on a Proustian experience, a sort of mental recall. My sense of smell hurled me back in time and place. For an instant, I had a flashback of myself standing on St. Vincent Street in the open-air market in Trinidad. It was sudden and out of the blue and it invoked the kind of experience that dreams are made of. A figment of the imagination, brimming with emotion and an abiding sense of loss and pathos. I suffered a sadness that was totally consuming. For a moment, I was paralyzed, as I stood there in the center of the isle, as someone lost in time. Flashbacks such as these are among the hallmarks of displacement. The immigrant is constantly beleaguered by nostalgia, recollection, and feelings of separation.

As a student, and after graduation as an employee chasing after the "American Dream" and living the life of an expatriate, I longed to return home for renewal. For Trinidad represented a place of cozy comfort, of retreat, as a way of escaping the demands of work and the need to be productive. In developed countries such as the US, productivity and profit are the hallmarks of the enterprise. And even though my acceptance into the body politic was not without its merit, for I had found relevance and value within the campus community, I felt the time was slowly approaching to make a trip back home.

CHAPTER 6

Return Home

"Perhaps home is not a place but simply an irrevocable condition."

\- James Baldwin

FROM PITTSBURGH TO NEW YORK to Port of Spain, I was returning to my homeland for the first time in eight years. There was something different about the passengers on this flight. On my first flight out of Trinidad eight years ago, when I travelled from Port of Spain to New York, it had felt like a family picnic with everyone sharing jokes and local news, as we flew thirty thousand feet in the air. We were a loud and motley group, which on occasion broke out into singing the latest calypsos as we teased one another in jest. Flying thirty thousand feet in the air, even though we were not technically on Trinidad soil, I felt as though I still was in Trinidad. For then I was surrounded by people who shared the same culture and upbringing.

On this returning trip, however, that sense of warmth and intimacy was noticeably absent. I sensed that as passengers on that flight, we all had some connection to Trinidad in a variety of ways. I sat next to a young man who was being deported, having overstayed his visit in the US by several years. Some of us were born on the island,

and some were the children of Trinidadian parents. There were quite a few young children on the flight with their parents. Many of us appeared to be working in the US and returning on a short visit. Some may have been students on break for the holidays. In stark contrast to my trip home eight years ago, most of the passengers, once seated, settled down to sleep or read. There was little conversation among the passengers. I thought about this difference in behavior and concluded that the lack of friendly banter reflected how time and distance away from the island may have affected the tendency to reach out to fellow Trinidadians. Perhaps it was that the separation involved developing new ways of relating to one another that were more typical of their new home in the US. That is to say, the friendly, uninhibited way we Trinis have in interacting with each other while at home, was not always appropriate in other cultures, and perhaps more importantly, may not be safe.

As I settled down for the six-hour flight, my mind reverted to the place where I grew up: El Dorado Village and those glorious golden Poui Trees. Centuries ago, so the story goes, Sir Walter Raleigh was on a mission to find gold in the Americas. As his ship approached the island of Trinidad, the golden-caped mountains of the Northern Range came into view. He believed he had found the mythical city of gold, El Dorado. What he saw were the golden Poui trees in bloom. As a result of an abundance of these trees in the village I grew up in, it acquired the name El Dorado.

The fluorescence of the Poui Tree, *Telebuia Serratifolia*, emerges in late May and early June with clusters of four to six trumpet-shaped flowers appearing at the tip of a slender stalk. By the time the trees are in full bloom, all the leaves have been shed in anticipation of this golden splendor. Towering above electric poles and two storied houses perched on stilts, were these lofty trees with their ample trunks, each tree with its gigantic umbrella crown, striking a vivid contrast against the pale blue tropic sky.

The children of El Dorado welcomed the flowering Poui. Often, we would wait patiently beneath the trees, hoping that a gust of wind would flutter the branches and release the flowers. The trees would then rain blossoms, blanketing us in a golden cover. It was as though we were carved out of solid gold, representing different images in a garden of golden statuary. Sometimes we strung the flowers into necklaces and bracelets or made imaginary gloves by fitting our fingers into the delicate throat of each flower.

When I was a child of four or five years old, El Dorado Village in those days, stood on the brink of modernity. The island was still under the Crown, with an infrastructure that was rudimentary at best, even after three hundred years of occupation by the British. Midway between rural and urban, the village folk lived without the modern convenience of running water or indoor plumbing. The asphalt road leading from the nearest town disintegrated into stone and rubble from the center of the village in all directions. Vehicular transportation was uncertain. Once during an election year, and for cosmetic purposes only, a thin film of bitumen was spread on the surface of the roadway frequented by donkey carts and bicycles. In less than a year, the road fell into disrepair, and soon the layer of asphalt gave way in disgust, to the dirt and gravel beneath.

On another election year, standpipes were erected at intervals at the side of the main road. The village turned out to witness the phenomenon of running water. The old folks were the least impressed by the hubbub and ruckus of the young folks jostling with buckets and pails to catch the precious commodity before it all disappeared. This older generation had experienced countless efforts by politicians to pacify an obdurate electorate during an election year. Worn and wearied by hardship and toil under Crown Colony government, their dour expression did not auger well for the future. They were infrequent and spartan in their praise. Despite their predictions that this fount was sure to dry up after the election, we young people continued to douse each other in merry playfulness and jubilation.

This journey home was to be a short sojourn. I was on break from work for the holidays. During that trip my great-grandmother Julia was forever present on my mind. I found myself pondering about the notion of home. What does home mean to the expatriate who has been away for many years and has established himself or herself in another country? Can the idea of home transcend borders? Does it cease to be the one unique place unrivalled for position in the emotional landscape devoted to the meaning of home? Can the expat feel a sense of belonging in more than one country? To the native, unquestionably, one's home will always be the one singular place that offers comfort and renewed vitality from friends and family alike. A kind of haven.

I also thought about the status of dual citizenship. Did it imply loyalty to one country more than the other? I grew up in Trinidad. I know that the frame of reference and world view I acquired during my upbringing and adulthood are fundamental to the person I am. It is the bedrock from which I can build upon, as I travel, read, and meet people from various cultures. Assimilating within an unfamiliar culture is made easier depending upon shared values with respect to language, political system, religion, history, socio-economic categories, and racial/ethnic diversity. The closer these features are to the culture I grew up in, the easier the assimilation. This foundation of nurturance to me is crucial to the notion of home and identity. It cannot be acquired any place else, nor can it be totally obliterated. Home and culture as primary source of reference are therefore foundational.

This first trip back that year was meant to be somewhat of a rebirth, a recharging. As I went about my daily routines while in America, I would sometimes reflect on the place where I grew up. With the passing of each year away from Trinidad, my memories of home were beginning to recede further and further to the back of my mind. The sensorial memories particularly were increasingly hard to retrieve. For instance, I found it difficult to recall the fragrance of the flowers in bloom or the sweet scent of fruit ripening in the tropical heat. I strained to recall the scent of the earth after a mid-day downpour, as it emits a sort of acrid, pungent odor that rises to the surface, as water seeps into the soil. The wake-up call at the break of dawn of the rooster crowing, heralding the new day, had become a faint sound in the dim recesses of my mind. Now and then I could recall, just faintly, the loud chatter of a family of parrots flying overhead at sunrise to locate a grove of mangoes, or guavas or governor plums. I have been away too long!

The flight in was uneventful until the island country came into view. From the air, Trinidad at night, displays all the beauty and splendor of the Northern Lights. She is resplendent and exotic with absolute majesty. I was excited and elated. I was returning home to family and friends, to calypso and parang, and all the accoutrements of a tropical Christmas. I was impatient to experience the hustle and bustle of shopping and food preparation, family and friends enjoying a day at the beach. I felt pure and unadulterated joy. Just then I noticed a woman with whom I had worked years back. She must have boarded the flight in New York. She greeted me as we were about to disembark, in a somewhat chilly tone of voice.

"Well, hello, you back?"

"For a couple weeks" (in my most careful local twang for fear of not sounding like a Freshwater Yankee)

"That's nice! Well, some of us choose to stay. Others leave for good."

She was referring to the brain drain that many third-world countries experienced after gaining independence. It was not the welcome I anticipated, and the euphoria I felt a few minutes back, disintegrated. Was she suggesting that I was disloyal to the land of my birth and that I had renege on my responsibility and was not worthy of citizenship? Did she think I had chosen to take my abilities and education elsewhere instead of staying home to help build the country? At that moment, I was once again tormented by feelings of guilt and self-reproach. I felt I was not worthy of being called a Trinidadian, for in the interest of advancement, I had abdicated the throne of nationhood. The old biblical reference to Jacob who had sold his 'birthright for a mess of pottage' resurfaced, leaving me feeling unpatriotic and disloyal. Silence was my only response to this increasingly familiar sentiment.

It was not the first time I had heard these sentiments being directed towards expatriates. In the aftermath of gaining independence, the people of Trinidad and Tobago, Trinbago, in the 1960s, 70s, and 80s, exhibited a patriotic fervor which was fueled by nationalism and the Black Power movement. Nation building was a priority with a focus on restructuring all sectors of the economy, which had been neglected under British rule.

The accusation of betrayal issued by those who elected to stay was directed to the men and women such as myself, who were trained in the professions abroad. Most of us were not on scholarship, and only through hard work, were we able to finance our own studies. This accusation of betrayal was seldom directed towards blue color workers, or the unskilled, who left in large numbers to work in the US and Canada as domestic workers and tradesmen. These individuals would otherwise be unemployed if they had not sought opportunities to work abroad. They were migrant workers who often continued to support their families at home and looked forward to a day when they could return.

Those who planned on returning often directed some of their resources to build homes or support entrepreneurial endeavors back in Trinidad. They tended not to put down solid roots in countries where they worked. The idea of home to them was that of the land of their birth, which would forever be paramount in their minds. For these individuals, there is no place like home. Those countries, in which they took up residence, were forever alien. The winter months were challenging. The morals and fast pace of living with its competitiveness and materialism, often did not appeal to them. Several of my family members belonged to this category, all of whom have since returned, especially after retirement.

For instance, my first cousin on my father's side took care of the elderly who lived in the Bronx. Her husband was a carpenter in Trinidad, and she often sent most of what she earned, to be put towards building their home in Trinidad. She made the trip back once a year to be with family at Christmas. Then at the age of sixty or so, she retired and returned home permanently. She was able to build a beautiful home and educate her children. She often expressed dislike for the winter months and the crime scene in New York, but they were sacrifices worth making. To her, Trinidad would always be home.

Many of us who were college educated and who took up residence abroad, were the recipients of this accusation of betrayal, and consequently sought other ways to make our contributions. Expats like myself who are working in institutions such as colleges and universities, actively recruit international students on scholarships. Furthermore, most of us assumed responsibilities as good-will ambassadors and when necessary, were points of contact for locating opportunities for market expansion of goods and services in the country we presently reside.

Another way we gave back to our country of origin, was to seek out opportunities for research in the field of science and technology in the developed world. At times, these opportunities might be the only avenue available to a foreigner to pursue research in his/her field of study. In newly independent third-world countries, opportunities for study in the fields of science and technology are not always available, as they require enormous amount of capital investment. As a result of working in a foreign country, expats continue to provide a vast amount of intellectual property that could be developed and utilized by the home country.

There is a vast body of literary works by Caribbean immigrant novelists who are domiciled in the US, Canada and the UK. These authors have established the Caribbean, including Trinbago, on the international literary scene. I wonder if they would have been so productive if they had not migrated? What is the catalyst, the incentive to write fiction while living abroad? What are the conditions that ferment such productive literary works? In the Caribbean, the publishing industry is rudimentary. Consequently, there are few literary works emanating from the islands. This is not to say that imagination, creativity, and sensitivity are in short supply. The performing arts - dance, visual art, music, sculpture, and theatre seem to be the more accessible vehicles for capturing the creative imagination and the cultural art forms that appeal to the local public. Furthermore, there does not appear to be a large market at home for fiction written by novelists living and writing at home.

Each of us, living abroad who has made a name for himself/herself, becomes an ambassador reflecting a positive image to the world of what it is like to be a citizen of Trinbago. I recall the vast amount of recognition conferred on Trinidad when V. S. Naipaul won the Nobel Prize in 2001 for his outstanding literary works. Further contributions have been made by the philosopher/historian C. L. R James and Dionne Brand, the Poet Laureate living in Canada. I also recall the wonderful pianist and actress Hazel Scott who was married to US Congressman Adam Clayton Powell. The talents of artistes such as Heather Headley, Grammy Award Winner for best R&B gospel album in 2010, Nikki Menage, and Billy Ocean are noteworthy. Would they have been so successful on the world scene if they had stayed in Trinidad? Their contributions to Trinbago have generated a socio-economic substructure that strengthens and undergirds the foundation of the Trinbago's national economy. Therefore, in this globalized world, the contributions of expatriates are unequivocal, foundational, and irrevocable.

CHAPTER 7

Family Reunion

"No matter who you are or where you are, instinct tells you to go home."

- Laura Marney

ON THAT FIRST VISIT AFTER eight years living and working in the US, I entered the airport in Trinidad to the sound of Michael Jackson singing "Beat It." For an instant, I had to remind myself that I was not in New York City, because just before boarding, it was the last song I had heard. I had this extraordinary feeling that I had not travelled for thousands of miles in the interim. This sensation marked the beginning of many such instances of phenomenological experiences while being transported from the *'here to the there'* or *from the 'there to the here'*. I was expecting to hear the Christmas songs of Parang, which are unique to Trinidad, or perhaps, Calypso or Soca music, heralding a change in place and culture. Instead, the sound of this American icon who has captured the world with his music welcomed me to the land of my birth. What irony! I believe that if ever there was a need for a unifying force that could be used as agency to bring the peoples of the world together, it would be American Rhythm and Blues, and pop music.

I have always found the 'arrival' aspect of flying to be exhilarating and reassuring, as opposed to departure. For me, the arrival is unparalleled. There is nothing like it! Consider what took place on my arrival. First, the touching down on the tarmac - what excitement and relief! I had arrived safely. For me, the walk towards the gate after clearing immigration and collecting my bags could not have been more thrilling! As I eagerly anticipated meeting my family, I tried to guess who would be present to welcome me. I hoped to meet my nephew and niece for the first time. They were at the time of this visit, three and five years, respectively. As I moved towards the entrance of the airport, I was filled with thoughts of affection and fidelity towards my sister. Then I heard her calling my name and I knew I was home. I was with family.

The kids were there, as well as my brother-in-law, who welcomed me with enthusiasm. It was a short drive to the house from the airport. As it was the holiday season, the house was decorated on the outside with a veil of cool, white lights. I stood for a while to take it all in. The overall effect was of a celestial scene floating amidst a dark tropical night sky. Then I was treated to my favorite drink, coconut water fresh from the nut. There was roti with curried chicken and crab and callaloo. It was kept warm and waiting for me. The house was immaculate and featured a new accent piece of furniture, as well as an added painting on the wall, done by our sister, Janet, who is an artist in her own right. My room was decorated in my favorite colors. My bed, piled high with soft pillows in muted tones, was occupied by the persnickety cat who insisted on inspecting the entire scene before approving my return home and settling on her high perch. My suitcases were filled with toys and books and dainty little outfits for the kids, scholarly magazines for my brother-in-law, and the latest James Patterson novel for my sister.

That night I dreamt of my great grandmother Julia who within her lifetime, could not have recognized her birthplace on the island of Martinique, on a return visit after many years. In my dream we talked of change being elusive and occurring without one realizing it. Slowly and imperceptibly, it occurs. One slight step at a time. At times, however, it could be abrupt and precipitous, as with the volcanic eruption in 1902 in Martinique, which resulted in the destruction of the town she grew up in, all signs of things familiar erased.

My visit further demonstrated to me how elusive change can be, that sometimes an extended absence from a place is required to identify the transformation that has occurred. In the days that followed, I discovered that many of the traditions I grew up with had ceased to exist. For instance, the custom of putting up a 'live' tree at Christmas had disappeared. When I was a child, my father would take us to the Government farm in St. Joseph to pick out a freshly cut pine. That tradition of a 'live' tree has given way to artificial trees imported from China. Sadly, there was no environmental plan to replace the trees that had been cut. I thought of the poinsettia trees which were commonplace in every yard when I was a young girl. These plants are different from the plants which come in a plastic pot and are ubiquitous during the Christmas season – even in Trinidad. The poinsettia tree, native to Trinidad can grow to five or six feet tall. We knew, as children growing up in Trinidad, that Christmas was around the corner because of the magical appearance of the sudden, red crown of the tree. These trees have all but disappeared from my island home.

Change brought on by an imperceptible transformation, or loss of custom or habit can be overwhelming, especially to the expat like myself who visits intermittently. Those customs that have been part of my remembered landscape, which I once experienced in my homeland are vital to my sense of recovery and placement. When they are altered through accretion of foreign elements, instituted by a younger generation, influenced by technology and travel, or when the old ways cease to exist altogether, I feel unhinged and bewildered. I recall while growing up, that I knew nothing of hot dogs and hamburgers, barbecued ribs, apple and pumpkin pies, bacon, and potato chips, that are now among the daily foods eaten by Trinbagonians. They have replaced some of the old foods that I grew up on. Every night, my father would stop at the local bakery on his way from work to buy 'hops bread' which according to the Trini lexicon was "a small round bread originally baked in clay ovens on banana leaves." The outer crust was crispy with a soft center. We ate it with a type of salted butter that was golden yellow and was purchased from the village food store owned by Mr. Chung. The art of making this type of bread seems to be lost to the present generation.

During my visit, it was also apparent to me, that the habit of house-to-house visits by the village folks on Christmas morning by the village folk had all but ceased to exist. In the past, a group of revelers would turn up on our doorsteps on Christmas day, beating out a festive tune with their makeshift instruments comprising bottles and spoons. In recompense for their performance, they would insist that they be given something to eat and drink, as they were used to say in the local parlance, "to wet we throat." That tradition has been replaced by the more intimate gathering of family and close friends for Christmas dinner. Also, I do not recall while growing up, the tradition of caroling at Christmas time. But on the occasion when I visited, there were several groups circulating in the neighborhood during Christmas week.

I discovered that the émigré experiences culture in episodes. Culture does not seem to pause while one is away and rebounds when one returns. New elements are introduced, while others cease to exist. One day, I imagine, there will be such a marked change in the culture as I know it, that on a future visit, I will not be able to recognize many features of the old ways. Even the Trinidad creole is changing. I predict that before long I will need to travel holding my copy of the local dictionary, <u>Trini Talk.</u>

In addition, the environmental changes that have occurred due to the importing of new plants and tree species have altered the aesthetic and ecological effects on the island's landscape. We now have species of trees that were nonexistent while I was growing up. For example, throughout the island, especially in the south, with a large East Indian community, there are tall slender trees that can grow up to thirty or forty feet in the air, which are considered sacred in India. The common name for this tree is Ashoka. In Sanskrit it means 'no grief.' The tree has a unique appearance with branches that tend to droop downwards and ironically, appears to be in mourning. I was told the seeds may have been first brought in by Trinidadians who had visited India. There is also the Mussaenda plant which grows to five feet with clusters of pink flowers. It is now commonplace in Trinidad. The seeds of the Mussaenda can be bought in the garden shops - as well as on Amazon. These two trees are new to the landscape. They are imports. I wonder, if perhaps one day the flora and fauna of Trinbago would cease to be specific to the Caribbean.

On that visit, I realized I was experiencing my return to my homeland and its culture on many different levels. Of course, there was the visceral, emotional response to being home. The joy brought on through intimacy with family and friends; the spiritual connection with the landscape and the intense feeling of pining for the old customs. There were feelings of nostalgia and moments of recollection as I traversed the old byways and side streets where I once walked as a child. There was also a response which involved the use of my senses. I discovered that there were touchstones which elicited a reaction to the landscape that involved the sights, smells, and sounds which defined my homeland. A visit to the open-air market, with the sweet scent of ripened mangoes and pommecythere or golden apple comingled with the freshness of the sea through the daily catch of Grouper and Swordfish and Red Snapper. And the voice of the peanut vendor, an octave above the din and noise of the Saturday morning bustle, with his plaintive cry of "salt nut, fresh nut, peanut get it here." For this was home. This was Trinidad. But for how much longer should I expect this to continue? I shudder to think that one day the open-air market or the peanut vendor would cease to exist.

The visit also marked the beginning of some insights into feelings of loss. Did my great-grandmother have memories such as these which she associated only to Martinique where she grew up? Did it all disappear on her return? I too found that during my visit, after eight years, some of the touchstones had evaporated, like the morning dew. Would I experience the same fate as my great-grandmother Julia, at some point in time? Maybe I would need to return home more often, to avoid feelings of disconnection with the culture and the landscape.

There was a time in the past whenever I saw a poinsettia tree, my memories of Christmas as a little girl came flooding back to me. Now these trees no longer exist in Trinidad. Those occasions when I ate a 'hops' bread with yellow salt butter - I knew I was in Trinidad. But the making of this type of bread is lost to posterity. My memory of a starry moonlight night when I would take a stroll under the tropical sky and smell the sweet fragrance of the Ladies of the Night Tree - I knew I was in Trinidad. Today, in Trinidad this plant is almost on the verge of extinction. This plant as with many others is being replaced by new species that have been introduced in Trinbago. As a result, I am unable to associate them with the landscape of my homeland. I wondered if my homeland would become unrecognizable. Only time would tell.

CHAPTER 8

Mother

"God could not be everywhere, and therefore he made mothers."

-Rudyard Kipling

HOME SWEET HOME! THIS FIRST visit after eight years of study and work in the US, was invaluable in helping me to further understand the meaning of home and homeland. I knew that a great part of what it meant to me was associated with my memories. The memories which were about the landscape, and of the culture, were central to my overall experience. Without these memories, I would have no association to the place; it would be like any other country I happened to visit for the first time as a tourist. It was clear to me as well, that memories were revived through certain touchstones, such as the landscape, flowers, trees, food, and common practices, and that when those were no longer apparent, memories could be so weakened as to disappear. To this end, I felt compelled to return to El Dorado, where I spent most of my childhood, until I was about eighteen years old. Furthermore, the need to recapture memories of my early upbringing, of my relations with the people of my village, and my schooling, was also essential so that I could trace and identify what was unique to this place, that it merited the classification, 'home'. It seemed natural that a quest of this sort should begin with capturing the essence of my mother.

My mother was buried in Trinidad, and for this reason it will forever be a special place for me. However, a return to the village of El Dorado was important as well because in my mind's eye, I could trace the comings and goings from place to place, of her daily routine. Although I had not been in the village for many years, I was hoping that my return there would reawaken the memory of who she was. My time away was causing these memories to slowly dissipate, so I felt I was on a mission to recapture the essence of her life.

I think of my mother as the embodiment of an anguished soul, far ahead of her time, trapped by the constraints of poverty, and held hostage by a lack of opportunity. I thought that maybe if I went back to that place, I could more fully understanding the daily obstacles she faced. My mother, of East Indian heritage, was the second generation to be born on the island. Her parents must have separated when she was young, as she lived with her grandfather, while her brother lived with his father. My mother and her brother were separated at the age of five or six and had little or no contact in the intervening years. Education for girls was not a priority then. She could read and write and possessed good arithmetical skills, but it did not extend beyond a third-grade education. Her brother went on to finish middle school. She often hinted that she had experienced abuse, but would not elaborate. In fact, she was taciturn about her whole upbringing, refusing to talk about her relationship with her family. Thinking about my mother's experience, I have often thought about the evanescent quality of memory and how victims of trauma and abuse can eradicate the experience from their mind.

My youngest sister, Mia and I drove slowly through El Dorado Village. It was nearly unrecognizable, for the transformation was almost total. Our family house had been torn down and replaced by another. The old access road was paved over and extended in all directions. Small dwellings were consolidated into modern apartments. The little hillock where we once climbed, had been leveled down to make way for a modern style supermarket. I felt the spirit of my great-grandmother Julia, reaching down through the years and caressing me in sympathy. Change! I was struck by how absurd it was to have allowed memory to be affixed to place. For places change overtime, and time, being the handmaiden of change can render a place unrecognizable.

As a child from a poor family, living under colonialism, my mother had little opportunity for education. Girls especially were the least likely to complete elementary school, thus perpetuating the cycle of poverty and disenfranchisement. As a colony, Trinidad was exploited under the guise of a civilizing agency by Europe: first the Spanish, then the French and lastly the British. Poor, uneducated women like my mother, were rendered voiceless. It was not until we achieved independence, that universal education became mandatory for boys and girls. By then, my mother had children of her own, with no marketable skills. It was too late for her. Her fate had been sealed.

My mother was not superstitious. Neither was she overly religious. She believed life was what you made of it, rather than the result of divine providence. She believed that accepting fate was defeatist. She had come to this realization early in her life. Her wish was that her children would not put too much emphasis on fate. Instead, she instilled in all three of us, the importance of a good education as a vehicle for economic power and dignity. Education was the portal to which she did not have access. But we did. We needed to grasp it as though our lives depended on it, and in many ways we did.

My mother shielded us from domesticity by being an organized homemaker. She preferred to do all the household chores. This was to ensure that we would not be distracted from "book learning." I still cling to images of my mother, of her tireless efforts to contend with antiquated methods of clothes washing, ironing, dishwashing, and of pouring over a kerosene stove day-in and day-out. For there was no indoor plumbing. She scrubbed, and polished and would get down on her hands and knees as though in an act of contrition. This was her penance, her "purgatory" she would say, not her children's.

My mother's homemade bookkeeping methods guided us from paycheck to paycheck of my father's meager income as a chauffeur. She claimed that his wages "evaporated into smoke." She bought everything on credit from the local shopkeeper. He would write the amount owed to him in his little book under my mother's name. At the end of the week, she would settle the account when my father was paid. Once a month, an itinerant salesman would drive through the village. He was Syrian by birth. He sold everything from out of his rundown, ramshackle vehicle - fabric, shoes, hats, jewelry, pots, and pans. In good faith, he extended credit to the women in the village. In years to come, he would open a shop. Later, this was extended to several establishments throughout the island. His children would be sent abroad to foreign schools and universities. From humble beginnings, he would navigate through the social ladder to finally settle in a community of the nouveau riche.

My mother was a pragmatist and extremely industrious. While she lacked formal education, she cleverly developed a small-scale supply-and-demand business, growing vegetables – peppers, flat and long beans, and tomatoes. She sold homemade jams and jellies, hot sauces, and relishes. All our clothes were handmade, being first patterned from newspaper which she would lay out on the floor and then proceeded to cut out a skirt or dress or trousers. This she would then transfer to fabric. She loved fashion and while she did not have the currency to purchase styles that were in vogue, she nevertheless resorted to homespun imitations which satisfied her appetite for stylishness. I recall she once made a dress out of black velvet in the mandarin style, with a high neck color and a series of small, covered buttons that extended from the neck to the armpit. When she wore it, she was transformed into a woman of the silver screen. For her hair was styled like that of Dorothy Dandridge, the star of the movie Carmen Jones.

My mother straddled the fence between depression and pessimism, for much of her adult life. Since she would never accept fate, the ways and means of harnessing it were forever out of her reach. Maybe she might have found comfort in an abiding determinism, or an all-consuming piety had she been more compliant and passive. But she was too sober- minded. Furthermore, she understood the deep chasm between the poor and the affluence of the growing middleclass. She longed for the comfort and luxury of the nouveau riche. She hoped that perhaps her children would make something of themselves. She would do whatever it took to break this cycle of hardship. For what is there available to the poor but to live vicariously through their children? She was no different.

I was about eighteen years old when I first noticed my mother's slow decline into depression. This was partly the result of abject poverty, and partly due to the drudgery of ordinary day to day living. The drab quality of her existence, that consumed and depleted her energy, soon siphoned off her vitality in her everyday struggle for survival. After years of enduring hardship, her stamina finally capitulated under the unbearable strain of poverty. The impetus to survive was no longer of importance. A general malaise was first observed, which later progressed into an unshakeable melancholia. No attempt to heal herself was successful. Her mind read despair even in the face of hope. Once upon a time, the prospect of advancement was conceivable. However, the glimmer of hope for the future as envisaged in her children was not guaranteed. She began to question her denial of fate. Maybe after all, destiny was predetermined. Consequently, circumstance will forever be beyond her control to alter and change. The adages - *patience is virtue* and *good things come to those who wait,* were hackneyed clichés that would never apply to her. She descended into the realm of fatalism, refusing to regard optimism. Years later, when we, her daughters were in a position to lift her out of her hopeless circumstances, she had already declined into severe depression.

As I drove through El Dorado, I lamented the fact that so much had changed. But I had to admit that it was for the best. Change was not new to Trinidad, for with each arrival of new peoples from different continents they sought to replicate the culture and practices of their homeland which they had left behind. For Africans under slavery, Mother Africa was home. Since they could not return immediately, they sought to bring Africa to the place they now inhabited. Then, after emancipation, the arrival of Indians from India, who replaced the lost labor force, heralded an influx of their beliefs and customs into the Trinidadian subculture. At one time, Mother India was their homeland. Further contributions to the social fabric of Trinbago were made by the inclusion of customs and mores of the European way of life by waves of colonizers under Spanish, French and finally English rule.

My mother claimed that she had no special allegiance to England as Motherland, and that she considered the Queen an indifferent mother. For her, the imperialistic nature of colonialism had always been present, with its idea of progress being directed outwards and focused in one direction only, towards the seat of the Empire. However, having been born in Trinidad, did she ever consider Trinidad and Tobago a place to which she owed a special allegiance? No. Not at all. Such an idea would have been implausible, since Trinbago was not an independent entity. Instead, it was an appendage to the crown for most of her young and adult life. My mother claimed that she was "a tenant in the land of her birth" and could "lay no claims to it." As a result, the idea of home to her was a place in her heart that was kept sacred, where there was love for family and friends. It was not associated with any place identified by geographic markers but could be experienced wherever her children resided in the world.

I was probably ten or twelve years old at the time when Trinidad and Tobago became an independent country. The leader of the nation-state made a profound statement, that became indelible in my mind. He claimed that there could be "no Mother India or Mother Africa or for that matter Mother England", since in the interest of unity there could only be one Mother - that of Trinidad and Tobago. And so, unlike my mother, I slowly learned to embrace Trinidad as my homeland/motherland, growing up for the most part under the nation-state. For it was the place of my birth and where I acquired my identity. I felt I owed a special allegiance to the land, for it was also the place where my grandparents were born and are buried, and even though my great-grandparents were not born on the island, they too were buried there. But in the deep recesses of my mind there was still England as Motherland to contend with since my early socialization had been under the auspices of the Crown.

CHAPTER 9

Our Mothers Who Fathered Us

My Mother Who Fathered Me.

- by Edith Clarke

WHEN I THINK OF THE women of El Dorado village, under whose watchful eyes I grew up, I can understand why such lofty ideas, such as to what constitute nationhood and homeland were never hotly debated among them. These were distant and nebulous concepts, far removed from the day-to-day concerns of making ends meet, that occupied their entire existence. Home was a special place in the heart which they reserved for their family. Besides, there was nothing nurturing about the Colonial Mother who thrived on apathy and neglect of her colonial territories. They, along with my mother were the torchbearers who wanted a better livelihood for their children, and to this end, they directed all of their energies.

The women of the village were poor with little education and were mostly common-law wives. Out of a sense of community and the need for information, the women formed an effective network that was incredible for its efficiency in relaying news. Sometimes it would be tainted with gossip and innuendos, but mostly, it kept them informed. As children we were aware of this network of connectivity. It served to monitor our behavior, and exact discipline so that no child would dare to be insolent or be disrespectful to an adult. Our mothers fathered us and were relentless in meting out discipline, since fathers were either working two jobs or absent altogether. Their motto: spare the rod and spoil the child.

The debilitating effect of poverty and lack of opportunity for training and mobilization lessened once we were an established nation-state. However, it prescribed new demands on the children of my generation. With this new access to education, we were expected by our parents to break the cycle of poverty. We children felt the weight of this responsibility that so much now depended on our success. We were expected to go into the professions to become doctors or lawyers, or accountants.

Dr. Eric Williams, the first Prime Minister and Father of the nation-state, faced the undaunting task of educating each child. Much needed to be done to build upon the meager infrastructure that was left behind by the British. The playing field was not level in public education. There were less than half a dozen high schools built by the British, all with a purely academic curriculum. Those who gained entry into these ivory towers entailed scoring high on the Common Entrance Exams, which were given each year. Those who gain entry were mainly the children of middle-class families whose parents took an active role in their education. Civil servants, teachers, doctors, lawyers; their children matriculated to these schools. Poor peoples' children like my sister and me, had a more difficult time gaining entry because our initial preparation was not up to par.

In years to come, Williams would revolutionize this system and open it up to all children. As it was, however, both my sister Janet who is a year younger, and I, were not even selected to do the exams because of poor grades. As a result, my parents had to enroll us into one of the newly established private Catholic high schools with a teaching staff of high school graduates. After a year or so, we transferred out into another high school, operated by the Methodist Church. This program was far superior. We performed well and were able to enter the University of the West Indies. My youngest sister, Mia fared even better because she had at her disposal her two older sisters to ensure she would be admitted to an 'elite' school.

I must have been nine or ten years old when I announced to my mother that I wanted to be a carpenter. I would never forget the shocked expression on her face. She broke down in tears, much to my chagrin. I could not understand her despair. From whence arose this misery? For many days after, she wore the face of a tormented soul. When I was able to muster up the courage to question her about her disapproval, I was told it was not women's work. At this young age I could not understand why some types of work were considered either men's or women's work.

The idea of wanting to become a carpenter had occurred to me, as I observed Ms. Dolly, a newcomer to the community. She was a small, wiry woman with an infectious smile. She had three children. She moved into the community with all her belongings in the back of a truck. At the wheel, was an American sailor, who was on shore for a few days, and the father of her daughter. He had bought a small plot of land and they were about to build a house. I had never seen a woman as adroit with her hands, and as skilled in the use of tools: hammer, saw, plane, chisel. She was an accomplished carpenter. I watched in amazement as the house took shape. She had some help from the men in the village to install the roof, but she worked along-side them with confidence and dexterity. After a while, I noticed that the women, including my mother did not seem happy with her presence. They claimed she was a bad influence in the community especially for girls who were taught that carpentry was men's work.

Historically, the idea of specific roles according to gender was a middle-class concept associated with respectability. It prescribed certain professions for women which did not hamper their role as wife and homemaker, while raising a family. It also ensured that the men would always be the main breadwinners. The role of the Church was pivotal in the overall functioning of the colonial government. It also assumed a moralizing and socializing presence to ensure stability, as well as to maintain a docile work force. They disapproved of forms of worship that resembled the old pagan habits from the African continent. As a result, the institution of marriage, and adherence to a strict moral code were sanctioned by the church. For the church frowned upon common-law unions and illegitimate children since stable households meant a stable supply of labor to work the plantation. The men and women, though more so the women, of the lower classes aspired to a standard of respectability which they observed among their upper- and middle-class rulers.

Regardless of what the church leaders had hoped for, the need for respectability seemed to have acquired different meanings for men as for women. Women adhered to the Church teachings of being a devout Christian, of church attendance and charitable works. But the men in the village thought more in terms of defending their manhood. They cherished their womanizing exploits and the number of children they could father, especially male children. Their capacity to consume large quantities of alcohol without losing control, as well as defending themselves were also key to the notion of respectability.

While the idea of prescribed gender roles was accepted by most people on the island there were, of course, some exceptions. One marvelous example was Ms. Shanti. She was a young, single woman in the village who lived next door to us. She chose to learn a trade, claiming that women's work was degrading. She believed that it kept poor women chained to the kitchen and bound to servitude. She could mix cement and lay bricks. She did home repairs and occasionally, was seen on a roof. She was also a skilled electrician. Women such as she, intrigued me for refusing to follow the status quo. Poor women who engaged in labor jobs were not highly thought off and as a result, village women were reluctant to associate with them. Since their aspirations for their children did not include encouraging them to go into the trades, they were very conscientious about whom they encouraged within their circle of friends. Ms. Dolly was not welcomed. Ms. Shanti's independent spirit was labelled colorfully, in words we children were not privy to. Nevertheless, these two women taught me about resilience and flexibility. My mother was not happy that I chose to spend my spare time when I was not doing "book learning" over at Ms. Dolly's. But she felt that it would probably knock the idea out of my head when I realized how laborious it was to be a carpenter. On the contrary, I learned some important life lessons from that illiterate, unrefined woman who signed an X for her name.

Ms. Dolly taught me that all kinds of knowledge were useful. She once raised a question to me about the need to be well rounded in my education. If all I knew was about "doctoring" or being a lawyer how would that help me when I needed to have work done by a plumber, a carpenter, or a repairman? How would I know if the job was well done unless I had an idea of what was involved in plumbing or carpentry, for example? Ms. Dolly taught that one branch of knowledge informs another. So, by extension, both carpenters and seamstresses shared the activities of measuring, cutting, and cementing or joining two pieces of wood or fabric.

One day we were told that Ms. Shanti accepted a job to work on a ship that would take her up and down the islands. She was leaving the village. She had found a way to break the cycle of poverty. Within a year or two, news came that she was in America working with an engineering company as an electrician. The women dismissed this news in their usual disparaging way. Some years later, when she visited the village, the women were hostile and unfriendly towards her. They refused to invite her into their homes and treated her as though she had the plague. We the younger generation, observed and wondered about this behavior by the women of the village. We concluded that it had something to do with sexual orientation.

The women of the village appeared to have a tacit code of conduct. Their support was for the members of the group who were generally housewives, mostly in common-law relationships and with children. A woman who chose to go back to school to learn a skill like dressmaking or doing hair was encouraged, provided it did not involve the trades typically associated with men. Stepping out of these defining roles could result in the loss of favor. They had a low tolerance for the unconventional. They generally were church members but beneath this sense of piety lurked a superstitious bent. They supported the Church coffers as well as that of the 'Obeahman's'. They were also suspicious of modern medicine and continued to rely on 'bush medicine'. When that failed, they sought the services of the local healer.

When I was a high school student in Advanced Biology and Chemistry, I was told that Ms. Elsa's young son had Type 1 diabetes. She confided in me that she was worried that she would lose him to the disease. She kept insisting that she believed someone "had put maljo" on him. I explained to her that if he did not get regular daily doses of insulin he could die. She said she did not believe in injections. She then sought the services of a so-called healer. I happened to mention this situation to my Science teacher. I was concerned for the welfare of the child and I criticized Ms. Elsa for her ignorance and stupidity. I asked my teacher if it was a lack of education that caused Ms. Elsa to choose the services of an 'Obeahman' over that of a medical doctor. She said that the choice was sometimes due to desperation rather than ignorance. All over the world, people prayed to their gods or used the services or a healer to cure themselves or their family. An example of this had occurred many years ago in Russia with the King and queen, whose son had Hemophilia. They chose to consult a self-proclaimed mystic and so-called holy man, Rasputin, to cure their son. And so, when Ms. Elsa's son died, I was less condemning and more understanding. I had done all that I could to help her.

The incident concerning Ms. Elsa's son was a turning point in my upbringing. At sixteen, I realized I had a responsibility to the people of my village who helped to raise me. As a member of the new generation of educated children, I considered it my duty to gently introduce new ideas during conversation, especially with regards to health care and medicine. Of course, this called for tremendous tact and sensitivity; for old ways die hard. But I refused to give in to despondency. This village was home to me. It was where I grew up and where I could return and be sheltered in times of difficulty. They might not be the best educated of people, but they were wise in many ways. Ms. Dolly and Ms. Shanti had taught me some important life lessons that I have never forget.

CHAPTER 10

Return

"Only in the agony of parting do we look into the depths of love."

- George Elio

AFTER EIGHT YEARS, MY JOURNEY to the land where my mother was buried, had been to recapture the native in me, and to re-ignite the memory of my mother and of the women in the village who helped raised me. It was to them I owed a sense of gratitude, and the importance of making something of myself. On this visit, I found out how important memories were in connection with the way I interpreted homeland/motherland. Moreover, I learned that it becomes increasingly difficult to recognize a place with the passage of time. With the changing landscape and the loss of cultural practices, I mourned the fact that I may not be able to recognize my homeland while on a future visit. With changes such as the increasing preesence of the fastfood industry that is slowly replacing traditional foods, I am fearful that one day my homeland may cease to have relevance.

As I prepared to return to the US, the contrast to the pleasure of arrival to the pain of departure was depressing. After an idyllic stay, there is the withdrawal with which to contend - the arrival at the airport, the act of taking leave, the adieu, the parting, and the tears. In addition, there was the painful, arduous, and distressing separation from a place of leisure, one that provided a distraction from vocational tasks, professional obligation, and responsibility. Back to the grindstone!

On arriving at the airport in Trinidad, there was a deep-down heartfelt feeling of despondency. A few weeks before there had been great anticipation and joy on arrival. Now, that mood was supplanted by tedium and a dull ache. The task of checking in the bags, hoping they were not overweight, reaching the gate, and the final hugs and goodbyes were so very difficult. My niece at five, poised and cool, fared much better than my nephew, who at three was sad and disconsolate, as he tried to make sense of departure and the meaning of farewell. He was comforted by his toy Pikachu, that bloated yellow mouse Pokémon from which he was inseparable. My sister ever steadfast and cogent, verifying my connecting flight plans, offered final advice about immigration procedures. Going through the gate and last-minute waves meant seemingly endless waiting to board the plane. I thought of the journey ahead, the humdrum, dull monotonous whirr of the aircraft and it occurred to me that although there is a spirit of the wanderlust in me, I would prefer to forgo flying.

Once again, I was leaving on another red-eye flight; this time entering the US through Houston. I settled back reflected on conundrums. In Trinidad and Tobago, I was a citizen but not an inhabitant. I could exercise my constitutional right to vote in the Trinidad elections through absentee ballot, but I could not vote in any municipal or presidential election in the country I inhabited, since I had an H1B visa. I pay taxes in the country in which I now dwell as a foreigner but not in the country of which I am a citizen. Also, as an H1B holder, I was not a member of the community, which is the right to

citizenship, but I lived in the community. I am in possession of a social security number and a driver's license which signify citizenship,
but I was not a citizen. I did not hold a US passport, so I could not
be a bona fide US citizen. Such were the apparent inconsistencies of
being an immigrant.

After an entire day in transit scurrying from one terminal to
another, I arrived at my apartment feeling exhausted and drained.
This feeling of fatigue lingered for several days. The adjustment was
proving to be difficult and taxing. The journey in space and time did
not accommodate for the mental and emotional disentanglement of
place. Physically, I was in another country but mentally I was still
entrapped at home in Trinidad. My auditory and visual senses were
still connected to the island. The scintillating sounds of the Steelband
orchestra, the laughter of children at play, the native twang with its
unique cadences, the sound of waves lashing against the shoreline
followed me throughout my waking hours. I longed to be back on
the island. In my attempts to relieve my melancholy and homesick-
ness, I tried listening to Steelband music. I read Naipaul's _Miguel
Street_ again, because it was so reminiscent of the times when I grew
up. I tried calling up my muse and directing it into a creative vein by
writing poetry. I had read somewhere of the widespread occurrence
of refugees and exiles who wrote poetry to relieve the pain of loss and
displacement. All to no avail. I was besieged by an abiding funk.

I discovered that getting back to my routine was one way of
climbing out of this feeling of gloom. I had been working as a recruiter
for several years and had acquired the role as 'mother' and watchful
surrogate parent to several students on campus, mainly students of
color, whom I had recruited from Pittsburgh and Philadelphia. This
role gave me reason and purpose, and even though I was not in possession of the coveted US citizenship, I felt a growing attachment to this

place where I could bring hope to young men and women through the lessons I had learned of escaping poverty and hopelessness.

To this day, I am indebted to a man whom I had met the very first week I enrolled as a graduate student, many years ago. He happened to be the Dean of Admissions, a charismatic man with enormous experience with young people. Many of our students looked to him for advice and direction. He was larger than life, extremely trustworthy, and well thought of in the wider community, and on campus. If one had a problem that seemed insurmountable, it was time to visit the Dean. It is to this man I will always be indebted for the opportunity to work in America because it was through his recommendation, I was awarded the graduated assistantship and later the position as recruiter. I will never forget my first meeting with him.

He was the first African American in a top administrative position whom I had encountered at the college.

As I reflected upon those early days on campus, my thoughts were of my mother and her dismissal of the role of fate in her life. I, on the other hand was not so sure and was inclined to keep an open mind. Too much of what I experienced in those early days seemed to have some bearing on fate. During the first week of my arrival on campus, I began searching for financial aid, when I was told that there was a graduate assistantship opportunity in the Admissions Office. I scheduled an appointment to meet with the Dean. When I told him that I was from Trinidad, he praised the success of Caribbean students, who over the years had completed undergraduate and graduate degrees. He also revealed that the Assistantship which was available through his office was due to a small endowment that was bequeathed to the University by a Caribbean student who graduated many years ago.

Maybe the whole quest for the meaning of home and homeland would have petered out if at the end of my program I had returned to

Trinidad. However, it came as a surprise to me when I was offered the position as a recruiter. More than anything, it reinforced my feelings of self-worth. That I was recognized as being of value in this first-world country of infinite possibilities was completely astounding. It was somewhat ironic, that I, a third-world woman at the metropolis, the 'epicenter' of the world had gained entrance into the 'hallowed halls of academia.' I became a believer in serendipity, the lucky break, a stroke of good fortune. I would like to think that this offer was more than a fluke or a stroke of luck because I had found meaning in working with black students. Maybe the Dean had recognized my passion. Once again, I recalled the lessons of my mother who did not believe in the lucky break but felt that hard work brought opportunities which could be life-changing.

I began to consider the nature of my interest in working with this community of African American students, both at the high school level and at college, to ensure that they continued towards graduation. And I saw a similar pattern in my commitment to the people of El Dorado Village. After the death of Ms. Elsa's son from diabetes, I felt it my responsibility to share with them what I had learned to improve their lives and perhaps to eliminate the need to consult the "Obeahman." I felt that I was indebted to the people of my village, for they had helped me to define the meaning of home as a place I would always be welcome. Now I was experiencing a similar type of allegiance because I was given the opportunity to pursue "the American dream." For this reason, I wanted to share the lessons my mother taught me, which resulted in my ability to break the cycle of poverty. I began to consider whether this was the beginning of how one can became attached to a place that was not one's homeland. Would I in time be able to consider this place my home, and if so, what would it mean for the place where I was born?

Chapter 11

A Lesson from Home

MY AWARENESS THAT THERE COULD be doubt about which country one should call one's homeland or whether the notion of homeland could be shared, did not occur to me until I was in my early teens. On those occasions when my great-grandmother talked about how much she missed the old Martinique that was lost forever, I began to take note. Even then, I did not give it much thought until I began to experience a similar kind of bewilderment on returning to Trinidad, after an absence of eight years. I was unable to recognize many aspects of the landscape that had been altered under the guise of progress. Within those few years, the village where I grew up had been so altered as to be unrecognizable in places. A new and foreign culinary taste had developed while I was away, and fast-food chains were appearing throughout the island.

Like my great-grandmother Julia, I was setting down new roots in a place that was not my birthplace. I was now part of a community with new responsibilities and allegiances. Could this allegiance give rise to a feeling of belonging where I could say, "this feels like home." Maybe it had to do with sharing the lessons and experiences of my journey towards self-reliance. What were those lessons I brought to the young men and women whom I visited in the inner cities of Pittsburgh and Philadelphia? They were lessons of hope through education. I discovered that the appearance of poverty in

America was no different from poverty in Trinidad and the village of El Dorado. Inner-city life in the US had the same appearance, be it in Philadelphia, Pittsburgh, Washington, DC, or Chicago. Regardless of where people lived, be it in a hut, a row house, a tenement, a shack or a reservation, there was always the impression of a community in isolation and neglect. It was a place where clean water did not flow in pipes, and electricity did not power overhead lines. If it did, it was sporadic and unreliable. Materials for road surfacing ran short, and playgrounds for children were an oddity. These were the spaces shared by the disadvantaged, the underclass. These places, wherever they occurred in the world, chronicled the hardship and despair of people held captive from one generation to the next, caught up in a cycle of poverty. Could the cycle be broken?

Yes! There is hope, though not for everyone. There is no panacea. Some will grasp the idea and see the value of education, while others will consider it a pipe dream. The idea worked for some of the boys and girls I grew up with in a poor village, where the mantra of acquiring a skill was held with the same fervor as that of a religious fanatic. I shared the lesson that my mother taught me to the boys and girls I talked to - that there is hope in education. But it must be seized upon with an unbending and relentless purpose.

Many young people I spoke to were not so optimistic. They shared accounts of friends and family members who continued to hold down menial jobs even though they had higher degrees. They hinted that getting out of the abyss of poverty was futile; that the ascent into the middle class was beset by obstacles that were ingrained in the system. I am often saddened by this loss of hope in a generation so young. When I reviewed high school transcripts during my school visits, I could read the despondency in children's thinking as reflected by their performance. To them, effort was pointless and ambition a pipedream.

Nevertheless, I saw myself as a sort of 'evangelist' whose mission was to penetrate this cloud of despondency and to bring hope in the only way I knew. As a new recruiter to high schools in Pittsburgh and Philadelphia, with large Black student populations, my purpose was to sell a dream and to instill hope. I felt that perhaps if they heard my story, it would resonate in their young minds as one which was germane to their own personal experience - one from which they could draw upon. I had a captive audience, and I felt that my message could be penetrating because I was somewhat of an oddity. Here I was, a woman of color, with a heavy accent which was unfamiliar to them. Maybe I had something to share that was worth listening to.

Sometimes I would address small groups of students, and other times an entire class. Without fail, I would be questioned about my background. "Who was I?" "What was I?" "Was I from India, or maybe from Africa or Jamaica?" My response was always the same. I could be from any one of those territories. I am half Indian, because my mother was East Indian, with roots from India. I am also of African heritage because my father can trace his ancestry back to the African continent. My accent is closely related to that of a Jamaican because I am from the Caribbean. I was born in Trinidad and Tobago. Of course, my next question was always to find out who in the audience had heard of Trinidad and Tobago. There was always a student who knew someone from Trinidad, which reminded me of the sweeping nature of the diaspora, and how interconnected we were as people of color.

Growing up in a household with younger sisters, my family was guided by the principle of 'hand me down', for there was never any money for new clothes or books, writing materials, toys, or birthday celebrations. Every day we walked several miles to school and back. Television was a luxury item for the middle and upper classes. Some days we were without electricity because the money ran out and our parents could not pay their bills. However, candlelight was our reprieve, and we were always able to get our homework done. We knew we had to stay in school and stay focused. The public library became our wellspring and access to knowledge. We read continuously. The rewards were such that in years to come, education had made it possible for us to broaden our horizon, and to acquire further knowledge through training and preparation for a career. I tried to impress upon them that they had a lot more going for them than I had had, and to that end, with some financial aid and a strong sense of determination, they could have the career of their choice.

Although I often spoke to graduating seniors, my preference was always to be able to talk to sophomores and juniors. Seldom did I have access to freshmen. But by planting a seed towards an interest in higher education from an early age, the likelihood that children would take ownership of the dream was more compelling. I was aware that many of the students I interacted with would be the first generation in their family to go on to college. This fact did not bode well for students in households, in which higher education was seen as a fanciful idea. Many times, it was never even discussed at home. As a result, students were less likely to be serious about their grades, since they felt they had no chances of advancement beyond high school.

The absence of role models in the community, of professional men and women was also a deterrent to the idea of education beyond high school. I was amazed at how many of the male students I spoke to had dreams of becoming a basketball player. I discovered that the epitome of the successful Black male that they identified with, was often that of a basketball player, as portrayed in the media. Girls were more receptive to the idea of furthering their education. I was not averse to suggesting that a student consider going to the local community college, or to a school where she/he could learn a trade. Trades have always been a viable option for young people who did not perform well in high school. Academics would never be the most suitable route for everyone.

So committed was I to this role of 'evangelist' for education, that I was in the habit of questioning young people about their future plans, wherever and whenever I met them. In my 'ministry', I was steadfast and determined. With uncompromising zeal, I shared the good news of hope for the future. Whenever I was at a fast-food restaurant or a department store, or while in the grocery store, the car wash or in the public library, I broached the subject of training and education with the young people I met. I discovered that young people were always very polite and willing to take advice. During my career as a college recruiter, I was able to network with teachers and guidance counselors who shared the same beliefs. Establishing this network allowed me to link students with mentors and counselors which proved to be an important aspect of my recruitment mission and career.

As I conveyed a message of hope and possibility, it often felt like I was once again transported back to the village of El Dorado where I grew up, and where I often shared a similar message to the boys and girls of my community. As a recruiter, it was tremendously rewarding to see my students succeeding. Witnessing their success at graduation, triggered a heightened sense of euphoria within me. I felt

I had earned a place in the 'Fatherland', since I had demonstrated a commitment to improving the lives of members of my adopted community, and I believed I deserved to be called a 'daughter of the soil'. On those occasions, I would say to myself, "this feels like home!"

CHAPTER 12

Uphill Struggle

"Life is about accepting the challenges along the way, choosing to keep moving forward, and savoring the journey."

- Roy T. Bennett

As a woman of color, it was frequently my experience, that I became somewhat of an ambassador for the Black experience. Along with my role of recruiter-*cum*-evangelist, together with a willingness to reach out to people, to engage in open and honest discussion, I often found myself describing, defending, and justifying "Black" behavior to my White colleagues. I constantly struggled to confront racist attitudes and beliefs.

My network of friends included both Black and White men and women of varying ages. While I am secure in my racial identity as a woman of the Caribbean, as well as identifying strongly with the Black community, my impression was that I was assigned a racial category by White people which was a sort of aberration to the norm, a kind of pseudo-Black, around whom it was possible to relax a little. I found that I represented places of cozy enjoyment by virtue of my accent and idiosyncratic expressions. I provided a space in which it was possible to experience catharsis. I became a kind of sounding board for White people who needed to express their opinions with respect to race. I was often amazed at how willing my White acquaintances indulged in self disclosure. Oftentimes, when the racial issue seeped onto the surface, in the media, in the community or on campus, I was sought after to provide answers and to interpret behavior.

Black issues in higher education as well as in the society at large have become an enduring legacy. For centuries Blacks in America have been on the receiving end of injustice and are no longer in a mood to extend the olive branch. They are no longer predisposed to soft-pedalling the issue, towards burying the hatchet, euphemizing, beating around the bush or tiptoeing around the issue of racism. For the African American community, any discussion of racism became futile and frustrating. It appeared to them to land on deaf ears. At the same time, enlightened, liberal Whites, agonized over racism, unsure of what to do about their white privilege.

The transition from living in an urban environment to an all-white campus community, in a small town was no cinch. Added to the covert and overt forms of racism that were omnipresent, Black students, in my opinion, paid a heavy emotional price to be educated. A popular coping mechanism displayed by Black students, of clustering together, sometimes became a source of anxiety among White faculty and administrators. One day, a faculty member and I were having lunch in the cafeteria when the inevitable question arose during conversation.

"Why are all the Black students sitting together?" she inquired.

I replied, *"Maybe it helps with adjusting to an environment where they are sometimes seen as the outsider.*

"But why segregate themselves like that?" she persisted.

"Think of it in this way; It's what I call the swarming effect – as when people who share a common interest love to hang out together. In this case the common interest is culture and the place where they grew up. It's a cathartic experience. If you don't see color but only the motivating force, you'll understand."

Another classic inquiry which I often heard and one which epitomized a total disconnect with the past was:

"What do Black people want?

The obvious answer was, *"Well, maybe to be treated like an American citizen with equal rights, equal pay, equal opportunity. Have you seen reports of police brutality? Have you been to the inner-city?*

On a predominantly white campus racism invariably rears its vile head. I recalled a particularly disturbing exchange from a student from Pittsburgh whose parents were both professionals and obviously from a middle-class background. He approached me with the news that he wanted to transfer out because he was "tired of racist remarks". Apparently, during one of his classes, there was a suggestion of Black people not having a history and were savages.

"And what was your response to this?" I asked

"Nothing," he replied.

"Well, it seems to me that you know nothing about your history." I suggested.

"Yeah, I know about slavery and all that." He persisted.

"It is more than slavery and all that." I told him that Africa at the time of the Middle Passage consisted of nations and Kingdoms with a well-developed infrastructure and thriving economies. I suggested that he needed to read Melvin Herskovitz's book, <u>The Myth of the Negro Past</u>, so that next time this issue arose he would have an an-

swer. I continued. *"Ever heard of Picasso? Check out African influence on his art. He first saw a mask from the Dan Region in Africa. That had such an impact on him and other artists, that as a result a new direction in art called Cubism followed and became the rage in Europe in the early twentieth century."*

"What good would that do anyway?" He asked.

"Well for one thing, it is important that you should know your history and another that you take ownership of it. Furthermore, we have a responsibility to the ancestors to dispel the myth of savagery. How about you get that book and do a report and I'll try and arrange for you to do a presentation at the next meeting of the Black students on campus?"

"Maybe I could talk to my professor in Sociology to do it as my final presentation."

"Great idea let me know how that works. Seek me out if you need help." I suggested.

"Ok."

"Oh, and by the way, it never makes much sense to run away from a problem. Power is words and knowledge is a powerful weapon. Let that be your tool."

"Thanks Ma."

No predominantly white campus can retain students of color without the help of White faculty. I soon learned that the challenge of enrolling students into a degree program at the university, for which I worked was a two-part proposition. Part one, was getting students of color registered and enrolled. Part two, which was the more challenging of the two steps was keeping them enrolled. It was an uphill struggle to keep them registered. Retention of Black students on predominantly white campuses is still a major issue today.

Since there were so few people of color on campus, we relied heavily on White faculty to mentor African American students. What was distinguishing about these men and women who served as mentors to Black students was their dedication and commitment. Several of them extended themselves beyond the call of duty to ensure students performed well in their majors. Others used their network to assist graduates to find employment and internships. As a result, most students with a little help did remarkably well. Considering that several of the students grew up in less favorable conditions and attended high schools that were inadequately funded, I was impressed by the fact that many of them refused to capitulate under pressure and surrender to a "dream deferred."

Some of these students had to devise exceptional ways of staying enrolled. For example, my first graduate assistant on campus was a young man from Philadelphia. He had obtained his Bachelor of Science degree and was enrolled to complete his Masters' degree. At the time, his mother and two of his siblings still lived in the inner city. His mother was experiencing some health challenges and he confided in me that he was considering returning home to take care of his younger brother and postpone his studies. His brother was probably eight or nine at the time. Fortunately, with help from his professors, he was able to move off campus and rent an apartment that would accommodate both him and his brother. He was then able to homeschool him.

One day I had a call from a counselor in my network from a school in a suburban area. She wanted me to talk to a graduating senior. During our conversation, I discovered that the young lady was an exceptional basketball player with an 'A' average and had reasonably good SAT scores. We were able to award her some scholarship money to attend the University. Given that she was my very first recruit, I took a special interest in her. That was the beginning of my role as surrogate 'mom'.

During the first semester, she had a successful basketball season and continued to maintain a good grade point average. Then I got a call from her apologizing that she was not planning to enroll the following semester. She was pregnant. Before I knew it, I was weeping inconsolably like any disappointed mother. Why? How? I felt I had failed in my duty as a 'parent' to educate 'my child' about the facts of life. I grieved about her decision, which would most likely consign her to a life of struggle. Being a single mother at eighteen, without any kind of skill was a sure prescription for poverty and hardship. It would probably entail having to postpone her degree, while taking care of a young child. What would possess her to indulge in unprotected sex? Did she not think about the possibility of pregnancy?

In my role as the Mother, the "Ma", I begged, I beseeched, and I pleaded with each-and-every-one of our freshmen to sign up for seminars sponsored by the Health Center. In my naivete, I hoped that I would never lose another student to unplanned pregnancy again. As the watchful surrogate parent, who gave guidance and instilled discipline, my mantra was constantly about the danger of unprotected sex and drug abuse. Sadly, I later discovered how widespread the incident of unplanned pregnancy among college students was in the US. I was completely unaware of how pervasive it was, and that it transcended class and ethnic categories. In years to come I would witness many instances of young women both Black and White having to forgo their education because of unplanned pregnancy. Sometimes, they were able to get back on track, as my first recruit was able to do after many years, but, more often than not, they were unable to do so.

I learned that in most cases unplanned pregnancies were linked to psychological and societal factors such as the search for identity and meaning, as well as the need to be popular and accepted. Relationship anxiety may also be one reason why our female students engage in unprotective sex with their partners. The abuse of drugs was also worrisome. It was a factor in the case of the absentee student who missed classes regularly. I once had to ask a parent to withdraw his son for the semester and to seek help for him, after I found that the student was using drugs and sleeping all day. I suggested that maybe the appropriate thing would be to have him sit out a year and find a job. Hopefully, that would be a wakeup call.

If ever there was a period of my life which was fulfilling and most rewarding, it was the period when I was a recruiter on this predominantly white campus. Every graduation ceremony, in which my recruits wore a cap and gown was akin to giving birth. When I metaphorically carried them in my womb, the gestation period was filled with anxiety and fear that I would abort and lose one of them. I was the surrogate mother, the 'Ma', the giver of hope when the occasion was needed. But at the same time, I was unrelenting and would tolerate no nonsense. They were on campus for one reason and that was to get an education and graduate. When I see them now, all grown up and employed, I am overwhelmed by a strong feeling of satisfaction.

Maya Angelou's notion of home as a place where she had found herself and her purpose for living, resonated deeply with me during that time. For I had found purpose. I had become the mother figure who, with open arms and mind, gathered her brood. I felt grounded in that new role of the 'Ma' who was willing to share past experiences, and to provide guidance. In so doing, I created a space which came very close to my notion of home. But it was missing one important feature.

CHAPTER 13

Connections

"Human connections are deeply nurtured in the field of shared story."

- Jean Huston

WITH EACH PASSING YEAR, I became increasingly rooted in the campus community. My work with students brought satisfaction and purpose. As a result, I achieved a sense of fulfillment. But was it sufficiently satisfying and cozy enough to suggest that I had found a home in the US? Perhaps not yet. I was employed and I enjoyed the company of my friends. At the same time, I had known that although I felt personally fulfilled, I still did not have the sense of security that came with citizenship. I had limited rights. I was vulnerable to the change that political whims might determine that holders of H1B visas were no longer necessary, and as a result, I could be deported. This rendered my ability to feel at home as somewhat tenuous. I still could not totally lay my head at night in comfort.

Nevertheless, I found comfort among a small group of female friends, consisting of faculty and staff who provided sufficient distraction on weekends as we gathered at each other's home for dinner, to read poetry, or to celebrate birthdays. I felt connected. We were, for the most part, a group of women of diverse backgrounds. We often discussed the meaning of home and what it meant to each of us. There was a general agreement that home should not be defined by physical boundaries or geographic markers but by sentimental ties, family, and a network of friends. I wondered what then identified me as uniquely Trinidadian. Was it culture? Was it my accent? Perhaps it was my passport. Generally, the sense was that none of those factors was immutable. The longer I resided in America, the weaker my lyrical 'twang' would become, so that one day my accent may be indistinguishable from that of an American. As for culture, in time, I may not even be able to identify the customs and habits I once knew while growing up.

I valued these connections I had made with my female friends. I am often amazed by how much women are alike regardless of upbringing or ethnicity. I believe that we women have developed a unique way of perceiving our world and that socialization in a male dominated society has caused us to have developed an acute sensitivity. Maybe there is a biological or innate principle at work which brings women together regardless of where they were born and raised.

I believe that through my connection with this group of women friends, I was able to arrive at a better understanding of living in America. My friendships proved to be a safe outlet through which I could share my thoughts and feelings, and most importantly, my anxiety of living on the fringes of society. Some of these women, like myself, were foreigners, with whom I could share feelings of nostalgia and awkwardness. My friends also provided an opportunity for me to express the self-doubt I sometimes felt in this competitive world of the Academy. Many of my friends in this circle of femininity were born in the US. We often discussed the stresses and strains of competing with men in the workforce, where women were perceived as being too emotional and lacking rationality. I am often taken aback by how intuitive we women are. My closest friends were the most perceptive and knew instinctively what I was going through. They were a validating, supportive force when my emotions were most fragile.

No topic was forbidden when we got together. We shared personal details about our broken marriages, about our sexual fantasies, about the men in our lives and about our struggles with food or aging. In one of our customary powwows about the myth of the weaker sex, I thought of my first mentor, and grass-root feminist role model, Ms. Dolly from Trinidad. She was a woman who never had any type of formal education but was a sage. I recalled the essence of a conversation we had one day, her wisdom remaining with me through the years and across the waters. It was a warning about the belief in gender roles and the acceptance of the myth of a woman's place in the home, and of being the weaker sex. I remembered she had implied that if I should allow myself to accept the notion that I could not do anything outside of the prescribed female roles assigned by society, I would limit my personal growth. Furthermore, she claimed that I would sink into a crippling sphere of womanhood, and forever be relegated to the kitchen, where I thought I had power. She believed that to be caught up in ideas of old-fashioned gallantry, which treats women as fragile objects was stifling, and would hijack any effort on my part to try new and challenging things.

We were not particularly a religious group. Often, we discussed the role of organized religion in our lives. I shared my experience of the function of the church in my village. I remembered my family attended the local Catholic Church. The parish priest was Irish. He was an irascible, old curmudgeon who seemed out of place in the poor black community of our El Dorado. There were other denominations such as Anglican, Methodist, and Presbyterian represented in the village. In those days, these organizations were more concerned with upholding the status quo under colonization, of a patriarchal male-dominated society. They viewed congregants as a source of cheap labor for the plantation economy. Furthermore, they hoped to instill Christian ways of living and to discourage traditional habits of worship that had survived as cultural retentions after slavery and indentureship had ended. I was disgusted by the unwillingness of the Church clergy to direct their attention to the pervasive problems women faced, such as sexual and physical abuse as well as the financial, and emotional challenges of absentee fathers.

It surprised me that many of my female friends who had completed advanced degrees grew up under hard economic conditions. Several of them shared the experience of having parents who were laid off at the same time as industries were relocated to the Third World. It was ironic that we in the Third World did not benefit much from those industries, given that those companies paid low wages with little or no benefits. Most of my adult life on the island was spent during the period under the influence of the IMF(International Monetary Fund). This experience at that time evoked some very disturbing memories as I was a witness to the ravages which an economy in recession can wreak on a poor community. The men lost their jobs, especially the ones who were regular wage earners. The women who did piece work as part of stimulus packages were also let go.

I distinctly remember the plight of a family who lived a few houses away from where we lived. The husband left his wife and six children to fend for themselves after he lost his job. One morning, the wife left the children at home while she went looking for work. The oldest girl of six children was about nine years old. There was nothing to eat in the house and they were hungry. There was a cassava plant at the back of the house. The oldest girl knew how to get to the root by cutting away the stem and digging a shallow trough around the base of the plant. She knew how to clean the tuber as well. What she did not know was the fact that it was not the edible variety. There was no way to tell. That day four of those children died of bitter cassava poisoning.

This period of economic hardship was also marked by an increase in domestic violence. I was on my way home one day when I noticed a man bleeding profusely from a wound from his upper body. He was trying to make his way to the clinic after he was attacked by his common law wife. She had been abused one too many times and decided to retaliate. There was some talk in the village, as well, about infidelity on his part. He was a club manager and worked for a meager wage. He was not taking care of his children. He came in early one morning having been out all-night drinking and gambling. She waited while he was asleep before severely attacking him with a machete. He fled from the house, but soon collapsed on the road and died a few yards from the clinic. She was charged with manslaughter. They had five children. Nonetheless, life went on, people endured.

Connecting to other women in this way was like nothing I had ever experienced. It provided a sense of well-being for me, which in the early days, I could only accomplish through work. Now, I had a life apart from the community of students and faculty. With the company of my female friends, I could relieve my anxieties and speak freely about my concerns. When my emotions were most fragile, and I needed comfort, it was to the company and camaraderie of these women I often turned. They welcomed me with open arms just as that of a family would, and I felt as though I was home, if only for a moment.

CHAPTER 14

A Foray into Romance

"Life is a journey that must be traveled no matter how bad the roads and accommodations."

- Oliver Goldsmith

IN AMERICA, FEBRUARY IS BLACK History month, a time when we focus on, and highlight, Black culture and the achievements of African American musicians, scientists, inventors, and historical and political heroes. Arrangements at the college had been made for the campus community to be entertained by visiting speakers and musicians. Randall Robinson, a well-known author, and activist was invited to address the topic of Martin Luther King's dreams. The following week The Jazz Expressions, a band from Pittsburgh, was expected to perform on campus. Brian, a young man who I knew from the days of graduate school, now employed as a faculty member in the English department, had enlisted my help to arrange for the band's appearance. The leader was once his high school music teacher and after graduation, his mentor. The two men shared a bond which spanned many years. As a high school student, Brian had been a "troubled youth." It was not the first time I had heard about the bonding ties between those two. It was a reverential and paternal union that spanned many years. Brian had been introduced to his mentor at a summer program. When the program ended, he joined the school band thereby continuing his relationship with his mentor. As a result of their deepening relationship, Brian went to college, completing his bachelor's, Master's and doctoral degrees, all the while seeking guidance from his mentor. I was fascinated by this larger-than-life character whom he called his mentor and looked forward to meeting him.

I was first introduced to him by phone. His overture was singular: He asked, *"Do you like jazz?"*

"Yes." I replied.

"You like Duke Ellington?" He probed further.

"I love Duke Ellington." I answered.

"Well then, I am going to play a song for you. It's called 'In a Sentimental Mood.' You'll melt on the spot."

"I am looking forward to hearing you play it."

"Good!"

My interest was piqued! I liked originality. I liked the timbre of the voice and the intonation of the accent. It was not a Pittsburgh accent. His picture came in the mail the following day. It was to be included in the design of a flyer, announcing the event. I was looking at the image of a man, handsome and bespectacled, with an air of intelligence. I liked that look of intelligence. Although my knowledge of jazz was rudimentary, I knew something of the connection with the Harlem Renaissance, from the early twentieth century and the Avant-Garde movement involving music, poetry, art, literature, and film. I had listened to some of the popular musicians before, such as Miles Davis, John Coltrane, and Duke Ellington. But I was no connoisseur.

On the day of the event, the band arrived, consisting of seven musicians. The piano player and the drummer were the first to make an appearance. They were cordial and somewhat aloof until they discovered I was from Trinidad. That was the icebreaker, for they had been to Trinidad. Their initial attitude of indifference transformed into one which was friendly and chummy. I could tell they had had a memorable visit and were eager to share some stories. I was amused but not indulgent. I knew the familiar drift of tourist escapades regarding island women. I stood waiting for the leader, while the band continued to set up their instruments. He arrived a few minutes later, and with an outstretched hand greeted me.

"Gemma?" he asked.

"Yes."

"Calvin Stemley."

"Hi."

I could tell by his expression he was curious but cautious, and somewhat reserved. I liked 'reserved'. He was tall and moved with confidence as he tended to last minute details before the performance. And what a performance! It consisted of an exploration of the history of the music, together with selections drawn from the songbooks of Ellington, Miles Davis and other popular composers. His exposition and commentary held the audience captivated. And then he tipped the bell of his horn towards me sitting in the front row, while he played that piece. That memorable piece! That day I became an avid fan of Duke Ellington. The Duke!

I had hoped to chit chat a little after the concert during the 'mix and mingle' at the President's house, but the ex-vacationers were too eager to relive their Trinidad experience with me. I made several attempts to attract his attention but to no avail. When it was all over there was a suggestion that a small group of us should go to one of the local restaurants for a late dinner. On the way back he wanted to know if I would ride with him.

"Yes, I'd love to."

"Did you enjoy my rendition of 'In a Sentimental Mood'?"

"It was ok. I especially like the way you talked about jazz."

"So, you did not like my performance. You only liked the way I talked?"

"What I am saying is, I liked your performance, but I especially liked the way you talked about jazz."

"I understand," he disappointingly replied.

I wanted to be able to expound about his music, to talk about the subtle nuances that made him unique. I wished I'd had the words to comment on his sound and his interpretation. I wanted to wax eloquent on the subject, to sound knowledgeable. Even more than that, I wanted to impress him. I yearned to have been able to talk about John Coltrane or refer to him casually by his sobriquet, Trane, as he is known by musicians. But I was a neophyte when it came to jazz. So, I kept silent for a moment and after a short interval, all that came to my mind was:

"I love this car. It's an Acura Legend, Right?"

"Yes. It's old. You know about cars?"

"This is made by Honda. Isn't it?"

"Yes."

I had recently bought my very first car. It was a Toyota Celica complete with 'pop out lights' and all. Red! I had done some research on Car Facts, on models and performance, so I knew a little about cars. On his way to the hotel, he was to let me off at my apartment. I sat in the passenger seat, trying extremely hard to be poised and upbeat. I liked his hands on the wheel.

"What do you do at the university?" He enquired.

"I am a recruiter." I replied.

"Is that so. Maybe you can come and talk to my students."

"I would love to."

In this confined space I listened to his voice and felt its galvanizing effect. It was low and slow and revealed a kind of weariness. The human voice can be a remarkably seductive instrument. Unlike a touch, which is tangible, but ephemeral, the spoken voice weaves an enduring memory. It can be summoned up at will. Notice how in dreams, the human voice can penetrate the subconscious so distinctly as to be rendered audible.

He was attentive. There had to have been a strong mother figure in his life, and possibly a father too. When we arrived at my apartment, he held the door for me while I got out and he continued to wait while I climbed the steps to my rooms. If this was chivalry, I was sold. I thought of Ms. Dolly back in Trinidad who warned about being inveigled into the idea of the fragile woman. At that moment, I did not feel helpless. I did not feel that my womanhood was undermined. I did not feel feeble and inferior. On the contrary, I felt acknowledged. Here was a primordial man in his most elemental role as that of protector. And I, as a woman, felt safe.

Calvin was expected to stop by the following day to visit with the Dean, who having grown up in Pittsburgh, was anxious to meet him. Calvin had been the music teacher at the Dean's alma mater. I too, looked forward to seeing him again. When I was living in Trinidad, I felt I was attractive. Growing up, I often was the recipient of compliments and 'cat calls', from Trinidadian men. Typically, they are blunt and outspoken on the issue of women's appearances. In Trinidad, women often derived meaning and knowledge of what men admired through the social commentary of the calypso. I was no exception. But apart from Hollywood and the fashion magazines, I never could get a fair idea of what beauty was to the average American male. It was easy for me to read the nonverbal cues of Trinidadian men or to sense their gaze, whenever I was in their presence. The American male was not so transparent.

The next morning, while Calvin was visiting with the Dean, I summoned up the courage to interrupt their conversation, to get a second look at this man who had unknowingly disrupted my existence of serviceable hard work and no play, which I had settled into. I was distracted by a look, a voice, a presence, and an attitude of attentiveness. Dressed in black and white business attire, I was careful to appear as the capable recruiter. His greeting was down-to-earth and matter of fact, with little show of interest. He displayed none of the usual scrutinizing from head to toe or warm handshake I was accustomed to in Trinidad. He was civil, and easygoing. Inscrutable, I could not read his expression. He was like a closed book, mysterious and impenetrable. There was nothing here, I concluded, no interest not even the slightest curiosity. Just a direct brief eye to eye contact and a phone number to the guidance office at his school.

I was a divorcee and not entirely naïve and inexperienced. I was familiar with the mating calls, dances, and rituals of the Trinidadian male. They are charming and inclined to be old- worldly and chivalrous, and very protective of their masculinity. They also preferred a woman to be aloof, as they enjoyed a good chase. Trinidadian men are more inclined to gaze at a woman from the onset in a flirtatious and appreciative way, determined to convey an interest. Unlike Trinidadian men, American males appeared to me to be more reserved. I had observed that they seemed to stare less than Trinidadian men, and they were more careful about potentially offending women's independent spirit.

I soon returned to my usual hard-working self and placed whimsy and any chance of romance where it belonged - out of mind. I knew of no scheme to avoid these flights of fancy. It was not the first time I was lured into sensuality by the sound of a voice, or of the dignified bearing of a stranger, or a surreptitious smile. Occasionally, it might turn out well, but mostly, it dissipated like the mist in the morning. I expected nothing to come of it this time and did nothing to move it along.

A few weeks later I was in Pittsburgh for a Black Conference. Brian and others from the campus were registered to attend. We stayed at a hotel near the University of Pittsburgh. It was Saturday and after the event, we were looking to take in some culture in the city. It was suggested that we should go down to the Strip District to hear an R&B band. Calvin Stemley was the saxophone player in the band. We arrived at the venue after the band started. I was able to get a seat close to the stage. He knew we were in the audience and on the break, he came by to greet us. He seemed more open and friendly this time. He hugged me and allowed his hand to rest on my shoulder, briefly. I tried not to hazard a guess about this new interest for fear of having my hopes dashed. I said to my companions after he had left:

"He's in a good mood."

"Maybe it's the dress." Brian hinted with a touch of humor.

"Is that what it is?"

"Yep!"

I always kept that little dress in my suitcase whenever I travelled. Of course, it had nothing to do with the fact that I was hoping to see him again. Or did it? After the gig, he insisted on taking me back to the hotel, claiming that "wherever I was going he was also." This time, I felt more in control and even feigned aloofness. We drove in silence for most of the way until the hotel was in view:

"When do you go back to campus?"

"On Monday"

"Do you want to get together for dinner?"

"Let's do a rain check on that. I am meeting with some prospects during the day. I am not sure what time I'll be finished."

"I'll call you later."

"Ok."

Once again, he made sure I was safe in the elevator before he left. The following day, after I finished meeting with several prospects, I decided to walk on the University of Pittsburgh's campus when I received his call.

"What are you doing?"

"I am walking on Pitt's campus."

"That's not a good idea. Go back to the hotel, I'll come by and we can walk together."

"Ok."

That evening we walked mostly in silence until the sun went down low into the horizon. We shared an occasional thought here and there and exchanged an occasional glance. It was clear that we both had experienced the mountains and valleys of past relationships, climbed out of the thistle and thorn of lost loves, felt the shaft of misplaced emotion, and encountered the occasional Cupid's arrow. Now we were not young, nor were we old, and as we continued to walk, we were aware of the magic and thrill of the moment. In the twilight, our shadows merged irresistibly drawing us together.

In my past, I had crisscrossed along the way in pursuit of Parvati, the Hindu goddess who is the most powerful deity of love. She was the wife of Shiva, the protector and regenerator of the universe. In my quest to discover the mystery of the feminine, and to divine the path to the ultimate male, I had read Hindu mythology. I found the story of Shiva and Parvati to be compelling. She was charmed by the essence of Shiva. He on the other hand, was wary and skeptical of devotion and needed proof of her ardor. To prove her love, she then chose to adopt the life of a recluse and the abstinence of a nun. Only then did he accept her as his consort. Up to that point, I had yet to meet what I considered to be the ultimate male - one who could move me in a manner, as with Parvati, to asceticism. My foray into the affairs of the heart was of a marriage which had fizzled out and fallen into decay, followed by other entanglements that plundered and exploited my vitality. These were all relationships with men who shared my culture. They wreaked havoc on my being to the extent that I drifted away from Parvati and adopted Athena the goddess of celibacy from Greek Mythology.

I was apprehensive about entering into a cross-cultural relationship. Although I was living and working in a cultural milieu that was not my own, I still had a lot to learn. I was taken aback at the effect this man was having on me. What began as a tranquil and calm acceptance, was soon transformed into an intense and absorbing surrender. Suddenly, I seemed to have taken up the quest once again to discover the essence of Shiva, by zigzagging along the way from one country to another.

This time however, I had a premonition, a gut feeling that the path before me was the right one. Although I was aware that intuition directs behavior in a way which is sometimes irrational, and did not often follow reason, I was prepared to listen to my instincts this time. I felt both harmony and symmetry with this man. When walking together we seemed to be in perfect balance, our steps resonating rhythmically. We looked good together and felt to be in the right proportion with one another.

I could not help but consider the parallels in our culture. In some sense, we were both from marginalized cultures, even though there was a difference in our cultural scripts. I grew up partly under colonialism, which programmed me to be loyal to the British empire, thus relegating my island culture to the background. However, part of my upbringing was also under the nation state, with allegiance to the nation. Then, I became a Trinidadian. I laid to rest my Britishness, slowly, but not completely. It was and still is my belief, however, that the Black American still struggles under a pervasive form of colonialism and more consequently, the scourge of racism, both constructs of which are bent on denying him a place in the Republic. I sense that at times, Black Americans seem to live in a state of limbo, lost somewhere between being Black and American. As is well documented, this tension infiltrates every aspect of the Black American's existence which is worn like a cloak to mask feelings of angst and outrage. Furthermore, Black Americans have every right to call America their homeland since the blood, sweat and tears of their ancestors helped to form the bedrock of this nation.

What was clear to me was that the matter of white entitlement affects me just as it does a Black American. I also exist on the periphery, along with the Black American. I was also aware of the myth of the West Indian being the preferred minority. In my experience, this so-called preference did not incur any type of privilege. We were paid at the same rate and sometimes lower. With this awareness in mind, I have often referred to myself as Black, instead of Other/West Indian. I concluded that maybe the time was ripe to relax my concerns about a cross-cultural relationship. It would be a new experience. There was physical attraction, for I could feel the chemistry. I decided that I would then settle for an old-fashioned, traditional courtship where he would take the lead and I would follow.

Several years ago, when I was offered employment to work as a recruiter on a predominantly white campus, I was elated. My work with students of color had brought fulfillment and a sense of purpose. The life I experienced off campus in the company of close friends provided a space to relax and unwind. All this seemed to draw me closer into the company of people who welcomed me into their hearts and home. On those occasions, I seldom felt the distance of the outsider. Now with this foray into romance, I again wondered where it would all lead. Was I headed towards a clearer understanding of what it feels like to be home? And would this put to rest the questions as to where was homeland for the emigre that my great-grandmother Julia asked time and time again?

CHAPTER 15

Paramour

"For the two of us, home isn't a place. It is a person. And we are finally home."

- Stephanie Perkins

CALVIN GREW UP IN CHICAGO, graduated from Grambling University, and University of Pittsburgh. At the time he was going through a protracted divorce. There were no children in the marriage. As the oldest child to his parents, there were also three sisters and a brother. He was part of an extended family of aunts, uncles, and cousins, all still in the Chicago area. He lived for jazz, as did his father before him, who was once a performing musician in Chicago.

There was a distance of ninety miles between us since he lived in Pittsburgh. We were together on weekends and sometimes managed a quick midweek layover. Every contact was exciting. There was contentment and gratification in feeling needed and giving affection. The quest was for true intimacy, one which would be based on trust. In his presence, I felt a level of comfort which did not require me to change who I was in any fundamental way. I did not feel I had to act like an American or speak like an American. I was a woman from Trinidad, and he seemed comfortable with that. Certain facets of my cultural upbringing cannot be erased, such as the way I speak, how I relate to other people, and my appreciation for harmony in color, which is reflected in the way I dress or decorate my space. Also, I am partial to Trinidadian foods, and I savor the aroma and the distinctive smell of curried chicken and roti, or crab and Callaloo. These are aspects of my culture that form the foundation of who I am. By adopting aspects of another culture, I will never experience a complete erasure of my essential nature.

Early in the relationship, while I felt an intense longing whenever he was not with me, I never lost sight of the fact that he was a serious musician. Musicians are a singular breed in many respects. Their instrument is their soulmate, unrelenting and constant in its demand. The time and effort required to gain proficiency and dexterity can be considerable. In the beginning, I looked forward to sitting in on his practice sessions. I was naïve enough to think that I would be serenaded by the beautiful love ballads that he plays during his gigs. Instead, there were scales, patterns and chords, the arsenal of a musician. Suffice it to say, I soon give up that notion. Any relationship with a musician will of necessity, mean competing for time and attention. It also meant contending with weekend and out-of-town gigs. A musician's partner unquestionably would need to be self-assured, trusting, patient and supportive. In essence, it would be expected that I would need to be devoted to the man and his calling. Was I suited for this role? Was there room for me to grow and flourish in this relationship? Only time would tell.

During this time, Jazz became a new, important presence in my life. I was perceptive enough to understand that jazz would need to be significant to me if Calvin and I were to have a future together. I was a quick learner, and fortunately, I was not indifferent to the music. I read extensively on the lives of the musicians and even subscribed to two of the popular magazines. We were in the habit of driving hour after hour, with no destination in mind while we listened to the masters. His extensive knowledge of the subject enabled him to identify musicians and their style of delivery just by hearing a few bars of a sound they happened to be playing on their instrument.

"How do you do that?" I would ask.

"By the sound of the instrument, by the technique, and their style. A good musician has his own sound. Sometimes if the musician is copying one of the masters, I may not recognize who it is immediately."

"Incredible!"

"Listen!" He would ask, *"do you hear the call and response technique during the improvisation?"*

"Yes. The trumpet player sounds like Dizzy."

"No, it's John Faddis. He plays a certain rift that's different."

"I see, and because of that you know it was not Dizzy."

"Right!"

I was becoming an educated and discerning listener and soon was able to recognize Trane or Dexter Gordon or Stanley Turrentine. He said I had a good ear for the music. When I was in Pittsburgh, which was almost every weekend, I started going out with him on his gigs. At the end of the night the question invariably was:

"How did the horn sound? Give me a run down."

"Well maybe you want to use a different key when you play Stella by Starlight. I like a more soft and mellow tone."

"Ok. I could play it in B flat."

"I like that you seem to be developing a unique sound of your own. I know you like Trane and Dexter Gordon, but they are copied to death."

"Yep, I try."

I gradually moved into the role of a music critic. After a performance or when musicians got together, there was the usual hobnobbing and fraternizing. The importance of personal space was then critical. I was comfortable mingling and making friends on my own without always insisting on hanging onto his coattails. I recognized that after a performance, part of the musician's line of work was self-advertisement and networking and the need to socialize with the audience. As a recruiter, and accustomed to networking, it offered me an occasion to meet new people in Pittsburgh. I would insist that he circulate and exchange greetings. I could tell he felt free and unencumbered by not having to worry about me.

I embraced all opportunities to be in the company of musicians. There was never a dull moment. I could listen all day to accounts of their shenanigans while they were out gigging on the road. Often, I would tune in to a priceless conversation on a description of the quirks and mannerisms of another fellow musician. I especially took delight in hearing the 'jive' talk, a sort of parlance and use of the jazz vernacular. The 'where's your horn at' for where is your instrument or 'give me some skin' for a handshake, or 'nice lid' for a hat or 'man you was smokin' for you were playing your heart out or 'am headin' back to the crib' for going home or 'in the pocket' for a rhythm section that played well together.

No one could accuse me of being remiss in my duty to promote the music and rhythms of Trinidad and Tobago to the musicians I met. The scintillating sounds of the Steelband and the pulse and tempo of the calypso were somewhat unfamiliar to Calvin even though he had studied Musicology at the University of Pittsburgh. From time to time, we focused the cultural lens on the society in which I grew up. These were times when I could wax eloquent on music. It often was the perfect cross-cultural platform from which I could launch a discourse on calypso. The role of the calypsonian as informant and social commentator, and an agent of change which was unique to Trinidad. Often, I talked about my parents and my family, of El Dorado, the village of the Poui and the women who helped shaped my character, and for whom I will forever wear a badge to honor their resilience.

The Thanksgiving holiday was approaching, and he wanted me to spend it with his family in Chicago. We had been seeing each other now for several months. He had mentioned to his parents that I would be making the trip with him. I was apprehensive, of course. I did not know how receptive his people would be to a foreigner. I was aware that our relationship could raise some concern. Would they think I was after their son as a way of acquiring US citizenship? Since this had happened to someone in his family before, it was a legitimate concern. I saw myself as having accomplished many things since moving to America. I was working, well educated, and could support myself. Unquestionably, I was devoted to their son. This journey would be a significant one. While I had been in the habit of celebrating the holiday with friends over the years, this was altogether different. It was fair to surmise that this would be an initial look-over. It would be a sort of trial run to see how I fitted in and whether there was harmony and synergy in my interaction with the family.

"Just be yourself. You'll be fine. They'll love you as I do."

Calvin's dad was a retired veteran. His mom worked with the school district in Chicago. They were a closely-knit family. He referred to his mother as his 'rescuer'. Early in his childhood, she had brought stability and direction to his youthful misbehavior. He was a troubled youth on his way to reform school when his mother took it upon herself to sit in the classroom as a deterrent to his misdeeds. She became a permanent fixture, claiming that he belonged to a house-hold with two parents, and she would not allow him to become a juvenile delinquent. So familiar was she among the staff, that when a vacancy as a teacher's aide became available, she was hired. To his father, Calvin owed his love for the music and creative impulse to perform. He described his oldest sister as friendly and outgoing. His middle sister was the quiet and steadfast one while his youngest sister was determined, resourceful and fearless. His brother also graduated from Grambling as a music major. He was a devoted parent to his young son.

The nine-hour trip provided the perfect occasion for an oral history of the Stemley clan with an ancestry that mirrored back to the Slave's Bill of Sale. It was a legacy of miscegenation and manumission, sharecropping, migration from the South and settlement in the northern states. As we drove through Ohio and Indiana with its pastoral backdrop, I pictured in my mind a plantation, and what it might have been to be a woman struggling with the responsibility to procreate and keep the bloodline unadulterated and unblemished. For the assurance of the survival of the race and the purity of the blood, depended on the authority vested in black womanhood. Nowhere in the New World did women in bondage under slavery escape the licentiousness of slave masters and the miscegenation of the race that ensued.

As we drove across country, my first of many subsequent trips, I thought of the indigenous peoples of America and their demise. Calvin and I talked about his great-great-grandmother who was Native American. Centuries before Africans were brought to America to work on the plantation, a different kind of holocaust was taking place. Native peoples were being displaced from their traditional lands and penned into reservations. Driving through Ohio and Indiana, I was aware of a sort of sardonic tribute, empty and barren, which was made to the memory of the nations of the various tribes. I noticed the names of counties, towns, parks, rivers, reservoirs, and lakes, all named after Tribal Peoples. Leaving Pennsylvania, we entered the Mahoning Valley, which was a Lenape word meaning salt lick and the state of Ohio, and Akron, both Seneca names. The Great Lake area and Erie were names of Iroquois origin. Ashtabula and Pymatuning of Lenape, derivative as were Coshocton, Hocking, Kokosing, and Muskingum. Delaware, Chillicothe, Piqua and Shawnee were places named after the Shawnee people. Chippewa, an Algonquian word, and Wauseon were of Odawa origin.

At dusk we entered the Dan Ryan Expressway, with its frenetic six lanes of traffic moving at breakneck speed towards Chicago. I tried to imagine this great metropolis of Chicago being once razed to the ground by the fire of 1871. I guess one could say that like the proverbial Phoenix, Chicago rose out of the ashes and was reborn as the hub of a wheel with its spokes radiating culture, commerce, industry, and technology, with global links to the international community by water and air. As we drove through parts of the city, I liked what I saw of the landscape, with broad tree lined streets forming a grid, that provided accessible routes for runners. I was amazed at the city's architecture. It flaunted a futuristic stamp amidst public art works, fountains, and portrait statuary, such as the one of Michael Jordan. However, Chicago was also the place where I experienced the coldest winter, with its polar vortex that bore down hawk-like and relentless.

CHAPTER 16

A Notion of Home

"Where thou art that is home."

-Emily Dickinson

ON THIS, MY FIRST THANKSGIVING visit to meet the Stemley family in Chicago, a welcoming party of siblings and parents rolled out the veritable red carpet. The warm glow of the house and the outpouring of emotion was reassuring. In fact, it felt familiar and comfortable, as that of a homecoming.

If home was a place where there was acceptance, one of approval, of acknowledgement and delight, then I was home. I was among family. I was in the presence of kinfolk. Now I had the brother I always wanted and three more sisters. I was fascinated by the affectionate rivalry between the siblings. Calvin's brother was younger and named after their father. His subtle inquiries about "our future plans," his surreptitious smile and teasing manner bespoke of a deep affection the younger man felt for his older brother. I was greeted wholeheartedly by his mother and father, who were jubilant because their son was happy. And I was glad and relieved at their open-minded acceptance.

This trip proved also proved to be a journey of the self, one which allowed me to experience a kindred spirit in a place that was not home but could be a worthy substitute. Did I feel a divided loyalty? Maybe. However, with regards to my relatives, my sisters and my father who were still on the island, my aunts, uncles, and cousins would never be supplanted in my devotion. They were consanguineous, flesh of my flesh, and blood of my blood. Trinidad was responsible for my heritage and my birthright and as the locus of my essence, it is enduring, and unchanging. Nevertheless, I was learning that it is possible to find value and significance in another place apart from my birthplace. And if the concept of home was a place where one is accepted and acknowledged, it may be possible to have shared loyalty, which does not involve a denial of one place to the exclusion of the other. This much I felt - that I no longer experienced nostalgia for my home in the acute way I was used to, and that the feelings of anxiety, pain, loneliness, and melancholy had subsided. I was beginning to think of Trinidad in a new way, one that identified me as an emissary and as an ambassador to the US. Thoughts of the homeland were now self-affirming and self-satisfying. Whenever I heard calypso or the music of the Steelband or when I met Trinidadians, I felt delighted. I no longer experienced the dull ache of yesteryear. Nostalgia for my home country was now supplanted by a new longing. This new longing was to be in the constant presence with the man in my life. I was not surprised to discover that nostalgia for my homeland which I once experienced, was similar to the experience of separation from the love of my life. For both were emotions of the same ilk, of a type of hunger and yearning.

On that Thanksgiving visit, I discovered that the custom of preparing the meal on special occasions was the same for Trinbagonians as it was in the Stemley household. It usually involved women of varying ages and stages of life sitting around the big kitchen table while preparing the meal. That occasion brought together five women in conversation, the four Stemley women and me, a welcomed guest. The conversation ultimately centered on Calvin and our relationship.

"Gemma our brother has not looked so happy in years. Thanks to you. You met on a college campus. Right?" his youngest sister asked.

"Yes, through a friend, a student of his, who now works on the campus."

"How are you handling the distance? He's in Pittsburgh ninety miles away?" his mom asked.

"I keep busy with work and my studies. I recently enrolled in a PhD program in Literature and Criticism."

"Do you plan to teach?" his oldest sister wondered.

"I am not sure. I do like recruiting. I like being on the road visiting schools throughout Pennsylvania."

"What's the food like in Trinidad? Have you tried out your recipes on Calvin?" asked his youngest sister.

"Oh yes! He likes curried chicken. And I make a brand bread that he likes. He seemed to like the way I prepare fish in the oven. We have some unique dishes that I would love to make but it calls for special in-gredients. I could do the Pilau which is peas and rice. I've never tried it here in the US. And oh, yes, he likes the corn soup I sometimes make. It's very much like Southern cuisine. You know what I mean, right, Mom?" I was getting used to calling her mom.

"Yes, I know the gumbo, which is rice, shrimp, okra, sausage and lots of seasoning."

"What's Trinidad like?" From his middle sister who was listening quietly.

"Multi-ethnic in a different way. I am representative of the two ma-jor ethnicities. Black and East Indian from India with small populations of Chinese and Europeans."

"I can tell by your hair texture you are mixed. I like your hair." Said his oldest sister approvingly. She had been a hairdresser at one point.

"Thank you. I like to style it a little differently."

"You should try a mousse. It will give it a nice curl."

"Ok. I'll try it."

I met the rest of the family during dinner. There were four generations seated together around that Thanksgiving dinner table. Between servings, there was an array of subject matters discussed, ranging from politics to economics to education, Black on Black crime, and the forthcoming winter. Finally, conversation settled on history. History in oral form, complete with the fervor and anguish, as vital as when it first happened. I believe that a retelling of the times from personal experiences are the most authentic. Often it was passed down from previous generations. I had a fondness for the oral tradition and so I was silent, not always sure who was talking. The older folks had the stage, and while the rest of us listened intently, it was obvious that their account of the past was not to be found in the history books. Neither was it taught in schools. I thought of how enlightening the discussion and sharing of their stories were. More importantly for the younger ones listening, it was hoped that they would learn something of their history.

"Henry Blair! Who ever heard of him? He was the inventor of the seed and cotton planter in 1860. Sure made life easier for Black folks!"

"Yes, and Madam C.J Walker. Before the Chinese cornered the black hair product market, she was making her own products in her kitchen."

"Who ever heard tell of Alice Parker, inventor of a furnace for heating? She was born when Frederick Douglas died."

"Did they ever find out what happened to the millions of Black peoples' money when the Freedman's Savings Bank closed down?"

"The Board was all White."

"Now why would we be so stupid to put money in a bank with no Black folks on the board to watch over our money?"

"It was set up in Washington DC by Congress. Who do you think would be Board members?"

"Ex slaves weren't supposed to know about money."

"They knew enough to save millions of dollars which was put in that bank."

"Embezzlement and mismanagement, they gave as one of the reasons."

"Bet you no one went to jail."

While growing up in Trinidad, big family gatherings were seen as something people who lived in big countries such as the US participated in. When one lives on a small island one is likely to run into relatives almost daily. However, with migration there are more Trinidadians now living abroad than at home. As a result, family reunions are becoming the norm. There now appears to be a growing tendency for family members from disparate parts of the world to come home during the Carnival and other holiday seasons.

The following day Calvin and I headed back to Pittsburgh. The conversation naturally turned to accounts of the family. We spoke of our parents who instilled in us the value of higher education. We talked about his favorite uncle who was an incredible cook and who tried to discourage him from pursuing a music major, since he felt that computer sciences had greater prospects for the future:

"I said uncle, I love music and music it will be. He was not sure that I could make a living as a full-time musician, so I made a compromise and studied Music Education instead."

"And your dad, what did he advise?"

"That I should follow my passion. Both my parents wanted me to stay in Chicago instead of going away to college. I am glad I did leave. I wanted to get away from home and parents because I felt I knew it all. They begged me not to go. They even offered to buy me a car to stay."

"But you left for Grambling. How did that isolated small town work out for you?"

"The first week I called home and begged my mother to come and get me."

"And?"

"She told me I made my bed and I should lie in it."

"And did you?"

"After a month or so I settled down because I was so involved with the marching band."

"How did you end up in Pittsburgh of all places, after such a great metropolis as Chicago?"

"After Grambling I did try to get work teaching in Chicago but there was nothing. I subbed for a while and finally made the decision to do a Masters' degree. Pit offered me a graduate assistantship and so I took it."

"Your uncle Bill kept saying you were like his son. How come?"

"He always wanted a son having had eight girls. He's my mother's brother and was a frequent visitor home when we were growing up."

"I like him. He's so funny."

"I think he likes you too. He said that I should take care of you. He thinks you are gorgeous. I told you not to worry that they would love you."

"What if they did not?"

"It would make no difference. I love you. That's all that matters."

"I love you too."

There were several subsequent follow up visits to Chicago after that first Thanksgiving. I slowly began accepting his folks as my family. Once again, I was experiencing a shift in how I thought of myself, as being solely a Trinidadian woman living and working in a foreign country. I was now in a serious relationship that meant I needed to think beyond my own life. There was no longer a case of me, myself, and I. I was now accepted in the family and had new responsibilities to parents, sisters, a brother, aunts, and uncles. I now shared their pain and good fortune. I gave advice when necessary and listened attentively when the occasion arose. I kept a diary of birthdays and anniversaries, amassing a profusion of greeting cards for special occasions. I made regular phone calls to mom and dad and often made the trip to Chicago with Calvin to visit them when they were seriously ill.

I perceived that the tenacity which had engendered resilience and endurance to function in a remote place and a foreign culture was slowly giving way to reliance and altruism. Now I found comfort in not having to always make life-changing decisions on my own. I rejoiced in knowing that I had the sympathetic ear of someone with my interest at heart. I felt that I could share the weight of the world, which for many years I shouldered alone. In the past, at the end of a long day, I would return to my apartment nursing a feeling of isolation and loneliness which I took with me behind closed doors. On those occasions, I thought of the 17 Meditation of John Donne in which he claims that *"No man Is an island, entire of itself. Everyman is a piece of the continent, a part of the main."* And in the stillness of the night, I longed to be "part of the main." Now, with this new notion of home, I felt I had become part "of the main." I was now enveloped with a softness and pliancy, that was focused on pleasing my man and sharing his family. I listened attentively to his advice and suggestions. Reluctantly, I traded in my beloved red Celica, the one with the 'pop out' lights, for a vehicle with four-wheel drive since he convinced me it was impractical and unsafe. He had me consult with a financial planner who was able to move around my portfolio because it was "too conservative." As per his suggestion, I even invested in warm winter clothing instead of unsuited, trendy coats that were useless in the cold.

CHAPTER 17

Marriage Proposal

"I believe that all our lives we're looking for home and if we're really lucky we find it in someone's loving arms."

- Anita Krizzan

IT WAS OF COURSE, THE most unorthodox marriage proposal. We celebrated my birthday that year at a remote Bed and Breakfast in West Virginia. There was a little balcony that looked out onto a garden, which was very secluded with a sort of rustic beauty, untamed and overrun with a profusion of color, unkempt but charming - the kind of garden-scape one associated with the primordial. Once upon a time loving hands laid the foundation for this English garden, with boxwood borders, ornamental grasses and a gazing ball that added a touch of whimsy. Now the overgrown beds of peonies, hydrangeas, roses, foxgloves, cosmos, and black-eyed susans, yielded to the hand of nature for its own symmetry and balance. Birds, and butterflies, dragonflies, and honeybees worked tirelessly to maintain order and continuity. Off to one corner was a crabapple tree. Maybe it was my imagination, but I thought I saw a shadow of a serpentine presence. We stood looking at the scene in silence. A dreamscape of Eden. He was down on one knee, asking me to marry him. I looked at this man and I felt like the goddess Parvati, at the moment when she agreed to be the consort, the wife of her Lord Shiva.

This marriage would be life changing. His family would become my family and my stronghold. My allegiance to them would be shared equally with my immediate family in Trinidad. Instead of being part of a small extended unit as I was accustomed to, now I would become part of a larger constellation of family members. I would acknowledge his parents as a proxy for my parents. On the surface it seemed no different from intercultural couples who marry into each other's families. However, our two-year courtship had taught me several things about intercultural relationships.

Most noticeably, how I communicated had changed. I seldom used creole dialect or Trinidadian vernacular but tended to communicate using standard English with American pronunciation. I relapsed into my colloquial 'twang' only when I met Trinidadians or when in conversation with family on the phone. If Calvin was present on those occasions, I avoided using the vernacular out of respect for the somewhat cryptographic nature of the creole dialect. In this way, I saved time in not having to explain what went on in the conversation. By this time I had gained a solid footing into the Black community through him and his popularity as a musician. Unfortunately, Pittsburgh unlike Philadelphia was not a hub for Trinidadians. Occasionally, I would meet someone and was able to share news from home. The majority of them were married to Americans.

Although I had accepted Calvin's marriage proposal and was delighted to be a member of his family, I was still afflicted by the childhood memories of women in my village who did not fare well in marriage. Once when I was thirteen or fourteen years old, there was a wedding next door, where my sister and I often played with the younger children. The family was Hindu and as was common in those days, the parents arranged a marriage for their son to the daughter of another Hindu family. On the day of the wedding the traditional ceremony began at the bride's home, attended by family and friends on both sides. Performed by a Hindu priest, there were mantras and chants to the gods and goddesses. The couple then exchanged vows after which the party departed for the groom's home where the bride would be on display for friends, family, and neighbors to welcome her to her new home. She would become a member of the groom's extended family household.

The bride, tall and elegant in a flowing white gown, appeared as a tragic figure. With downcast eyes she neither spoke nor smiled. The first time I heard her crying was a week or so after the wedding. It was a very disturbing and agonizing sort of cry as though someone had died. On one other occasion she locked herself in a room and refused to eat. She then tried to slash her wrist. The groom, anxious and determined to make a go of the marriage, and to save face in the community, thought he could use physical force to bend her into submission. But she refused to settle down as a good daughter-in-law. After a month, he gave up in desperation and his family took her back to her parents' home.

This incident remained with me because at the time my senior high school class was reading William Shakespeare's *Midsummer Night's Dream*. At the beginning of the play Egeus, the father of Hermia had arranged a marriage for his daughter to wed Demetrius. Hermia refused to accept her father's choice of a husband because she loved Lysander. They then brought the matter before Theseus, the Duke who reminded Hermia of the 'ancient privilege of Athens' which stated that a father could kill his daughter if she refused to marry according to his wishes. According to Theseus, her father was to be considered "as a god" and "one to whom you are as a form of wax." Suffice it to say that the female students in the class did not take this very lightly and a discussion of arranged marriages as an institution ensued. Although this was not the case in Trinidad, girls in India even today have been known to suffer a state worse than death through the acid bath, that can severely disfigure their appearance if they refuse to be a participant to an arranged marriage.

These two experiences were so distressing that I was determined never to get married. By age twenty-one, however, I laid to rest some of the fear and anxiety of marriage. I then married a man several years my senior. Maybe I still heard the cry of a woman who was yoked to a man she did not love. I thought I did the right thing by marrying for the first time for security and protection. But I did not bargain on being stifled into domesticity.

With Calvin, although I was sweet on the idea of marriage, I did not once suggest it. I decided to let things take a natural course. If it was fated, then let it be. If not, I was not in the least put out about cohabiting. For the texture of love was upon me, like an attire which I wore every day. I marveled about this. My approach to our relationship was always one of leader/follower. It was the perfect game plan. He did not feel pressured and my work of travelling while recruiting, together with his work of teaching and gigging contributed to a relaxing and satisfying relationship. I was comfortable with the state of things. He, on the other hand, had different ideas about living together. He later said that the mere fact he was planning to invest in purchasing a home with someone was a sure enough sign that he was ready to commit to a marriage. The date was set for later that year to take place the Saturday before Thanksgiving.

He loved the small-town atmosphere, so we decided to get married in a beautiful Presbyterian church not too far from the campus. It was ninety miles from Pittsburgh. We were hoping it would not be too difficult for our guests to travel to. I was to take care of sending out the invitations. We settled on five bridesmaids and groomsmen. The reception would take place at a nearby restaurant which was very quaint and rustic. My sister would fly in to be my matron of honor and his family would come in from Chicago. His favorite uncle would give me away. We would have about eighty guests.

One night in August, while I was preparing for my Comprehensive exams that were to take place the following week, he called me from Pittsburgh to tell me that he had arranged for the tuxedos for the groomsmen. He wanted to know how I was proceeding with my arrangements. I was not. I was so inundated with work and studies that I kept pushing back the planning. The invitations were still to be sent out. I had no idea about bridesmaids' dresses. I could not make up my mind about whether I should wear a business suit or a dress, short or long, or a bridal gown. Then he suggested I should call his sister who was to be in the wedding party and have her offer some ideas for dresses for the bridesmaids. She was then working at J C Penney. That proved to be the impetus I needed. She came through with some marvelous suggestions and took care of that aspect of my planning. Then I was able to move along with the invitations that reflected the color scheme.

That very weekend, I enlisted the help of another of my bridesmaids to help me choose a dress. We made a trip to Erie, Pennsylvania, a town noted for its wedding shops. I was able to try on several bridal gowns. I finally settled on one which was a light peach color with a fairly long train. I would wear a shoulder-length veil with a delicate crown of roses. The next week, I received a call from one of my friends in Pittsburgh who volunteered to be my wedding planner. A wonderful, elegant woman who was the epitome of high class and culture, she knew exactly what was to be done. She was able to step in and relieve me of the tension and anxiety that accompanies planning for a wedding in a short space of time and on a shoe-string budget. Her son was one of my early recruits who I first met, at a recognition dinner for scholarship recipients. I was so impressed by his confidence and eloquence that I approached him about his plans for college in my usual role of 'evangelist' for education on that very occasion.

The week of the wedding, I was expecting my youngest sister to fly in from Port of Spain to be my matron of honor. It would be the first time a member of my family would meet my husband-to-be. I was excited and ran towards her as she casually waited for her bags to be loaded off the plane. Calvin stood by taking it all in as she greeted him with the news that he was fortunate to be marrying the best of the three sisters.

"Make sure you take care of my sister because she is the best of all three of us."

"Don't worry, I plan to. I feel honored."

"Good! Keep it that way."

She was fifteen years younger and far more fearless and undaunted than I could ever be. She was candid, never failing to call a spade a spade. As the mother of two young children, she had grown up at a different time and barely experienced life under a colonial regime. Her generation was nationalistic and far more cognizant of world politics and hegemonic powder to the extent that the coup of 1990 in Trinidad garnered a strong feeling of distrust for US intervention when it occurred.

The consensus among Trinidadians was that they could take care of internal strife and did not need a foreign power to meddle into the affairs of state. She had attended one of the best schools on the island and travelled far more widely than I had been at her age. She was to stay with me at my apartment and help to finalize plans for the wedding. Being an interior designer, she undertook to supervise the decoration of the reception hall and to coordinate final arrangements for the church service. She would be the sole representative of my family, since my mother was no longer with us, and my father was not in possession of a passport since he had never travelled out of the island. Unfortunately, my sister in England, was not able to make the trip because of health reasons.

CHAPTER 18

Wedding Day

"Together is a beautiful place to be."

- Unknown

MY WEDDING DAY WAS BEAUTIFUL. The sun was out and the temperature was unseasonably mild for November. The altar was decorated with an abundance of fresh tropical flowers– anthuriums and orchids with Boston ferns. A profusion of white frothy tulle at the handrail and fashioned into bows that hung from each pew complimented the white aisle runner leading to the altar. The overall effect was of the appearance of a pathway leading to a tropical island. The groom and groomsmen were elegant in white tuxedos, while the bridesmaids and matron of honor looked resplendent in aquamarine gowns, a reflection of the tropical waters of the Caribbean Sea. The groom's mother was also clad in the same color as the bridesmaids with matching pumps. During the processional, the groom in his usual matchless and inimitable fashion rendered a saxophone tribute to the tune of *The Lord's Prayer* as the bridesmaids and groomsmen made their way down the aisle to take up their positions at the altar. The matron of honor and the best man then followed. We had chosen the Ave Maria to be sung during the entrance of the bride.

A few minutes before I was due to walk down the aisle, I began to feel panicky. I had not discussed with my husband-to-be what I had decided to wear. I prayed that he would be happy with my choice. As I was led down the aisle on the arms of his uncle, I immediately looked to him for signs of approval and was delighted that his expression seemed to register pleasant surprise. Only then was I able to relax a little. My Chicago family was in attendance having travelled the day before, all except my brother-in-law whom I later found out had car problems. Nevertheless, he made it to the reception. Calvin's elderly cousin, Isadore and his wife took a train to Erie and then a bus to Clarion to surprise us at the wedding. And it was indeed a pleasant surprise, since we were not expecting them to make the trip which we felt might have been too strenuous for them. My friends in Pittsburgh and on campus, my boss and co-workers, everyone showed up to celebrate the occasion of our marriage. I felt such a deep sense of gratitude that it was difficult holding back the tears.

I was happy I had chosen the Ave Maria. What majesty! I felt regal in that gown with the long train as I was being escorted down the aisle. I am ready, I thought. I have never been more certain of my decision to marry Calvin, I thought. I was glad that we had decided on a traditional church ceremony. Both of us had been married before in the presence of a Justice of the Peace. When I broke the news to the office that I would be getting married and needed a Pastor, my boss suggested his cousin who had recently been ordained as an Episcopalian minister. It would be his first wedding ceremony. The music, the walk down the aisle, the bridesmaids and their groomsmen, the candles - what could be more ceremonial and grand!

Seeing my husband-to-be at the alter waiting to receive my hand in marriage was one of the most unforgettable images - one which I love to recall from time to time. Of course, the most memorable occasion was the actual exchange of vows, which we wrote together. This marriage ceremony was also to be a commemoration of the passing of my mother, one in which we would celebrate her transition from life into darkness. The lighting of a symbolic candle was to invoke her memory and to personify the significance of light to represent a new beginning. It was an occasion suffused with pathos, while at the same time imbued with happiness and delight. When my sister and I lit the symbolic candle there was such a feeling of sadness that it was difficult to hold back the tears. I have often felt that had she been able to meet my husband she would have approved of him.

Following the Blessing was the Presentation and then the Recessional. We stopped momentarily to embrace his parents and to thank those guests from Pittsburgh who could not stay for the reception. For the wedding had taken place in Clarion which was 90 miles away. In grand style, we boarded the limo which took us to the reception hall in a little nearby town with a rustic wooden interior and wonderful fireplace.

My sister had tastefully decorated in the colors of the wedding party with little favors and lots of poinsettias to herald the Christmas season. There was a live jazz band during the reception. They were some of Calvin's students who had formed a group for the occasion. A DJ would play our special song, Stevie Wonder's *Ribbon in the Sky*, as we took to the dance floor. And then we would "break loose" to Caribbean Queen by Billy Ocean. Billy is a Trinidadian.

On that special day in the company of close friends and family, my husband and I were delighted to receive the many toasts for a happy future. I was extremely proud of my little sister as she led the toasts. I thought how she had matured into a self-confident and beautiful woman. After the wedding, the entire bridal party would drive down to Pittsburgh to be entertained by my husband's R&B

band with him on saxophone. I decided to wear the gown, minus the train, of course.

We settled on Puerto Rico for our honeymoon. Several days after the wedding my sister boarded a plane for Trinidad, as we made our departure to San Juan which would mark our maiden voyage together. This was an occasion when my left brain, forever the metaphorical thinker, took the reins of my thoughts. I perceived this maiden voyage as symbolic of the first steps we were taking into a future life together. As I settled down in my seat next to my husband, I clasped his hand in a silent prayer of blessing for the future and divine guidance in our marriage. I was reminded of the last trip I made alone on my return from Trinidad, after an eight-year absence. It was attended by loneliness and nostalgia which I felt for several days after boarding a flight to the US. This time I was filled with happiness and anticipation and looked forward to exploring Puerto Rico with my husband.

CHAPTER 19

Sisterly Advice

"Help one another is part of the religion of sisterhood."

-Louisa May Alcott

BEFORE SHE LEFT FOR HOME, my younger sister and I engaged in a heartfelt discussion about life, marriage, and family:

"How do you feel now that you are married?" she asked.

"Relieved. I was praying all along that everything would go fine, and it did thanks to some wonderful people including yourself."

"You deserve a nice wedding and a good man."

"I think I learned something in the interim after my first attempt at marriage. We had two years to figure out what would be our needs, our likes and dislikes." I replied.

"You know Gem, I discovered that the bond of matrimony is like no other. It is a three-pronged relationship between two people of their spiritual, emotional, and physical nature. The physical is the least worrisome of the three."

"How's that?" I asked

"Because the spiritual and emotional are intangibles, much greater thought and deliberation have to be paid towards ensuring that those needs are taken care of."

133

"Yes. That's a good point. I could tell you one thing I learned. The domineering wife/husband is doomed to failure as far as both of us are concerned. Also, the needy wife/husband who requires constant validation, is super sensitive and possessive will never work either in our marriage." I said.

"That was my problem in my first marriage. The domineering husband, and a family that felt he was too good for me," she confided.

"Mine was marrying for the wrong reason. I wanted a father figure more so than a husband because I was so scared of marriage and commitment"

"I think you have found your soulmate. You will be all right."

"Thanks Sis. I am glad you also have found a good man who cherishes you. You have two beautiful kids. You deserve it."

"It was a beautiful wedding."

"Yes, I am happy it turned out well."

I felt confident about my marriage since I was more assured of myself than ever before. I had learned a few ways to handle the spiritual and emotional aspects which my sister had referred to. I was always a firm believer in my responsibility to structure my own time and not having to depend solely on a mate or companion to always fulfill my emotional needs. As a result, I kept busy with my work and studies. I also had a small circle of friends whose interest in the theatre and literary pursuits I shared. From the onset of our relationship, I discovered the unique mindset and independence of musicians and their need for space. I tried to honor this as much as possible.

However, while I relished independence, I soon learned that there was a fine line between reliance and independence. I had to check myself on many occasions when I was inclined to make decisions on my own without seeking the support and advice of the man in my life. When things backfired, I would then come running to him with my tail between my legs. I knew this was an area I had to work on. I was happy in knowing that he was not domineering or autocratic. But at the same time, he was no pushover. God forbid if I tried to urge him into making a decision, when he was not ready. In those instances, he would morph into a stubborn mule.

There is an aspect of who I am that is deeply rooted in my psyche as to be almost innate. I need also to keep that under wraps. It is the tendency to be too nurturing. It is not exactly a cowering or cringing or being at his beck and call in a somewhat slavish or ingratiating manner, but of a propensity to defer my immediate game plan, my own personal needs, my course of action or undertaking, to take care of his needs. In the beginning of our relationship, he chided me for doing so in a somewhat amicable tone, claiming that he could take care of himself and that I should relax.

After a while, I realized that the initial upbraiding was being transformed into an acceptance and satisfaction with progressively little resistance on his part. I recognized that he decided to excuse this tendency in me as being of a Southern 'thang' or a Caribbean thing. It was not a trait I was deeply anxious to abandon, for I realized that it triggered an acute sense of altruism in him. Not that he was entirely selfish, but his instrument was once his focus; by the time of his proposal, he had come to jettison that idea. Furthermore, this Southern 'thang' was truly an affirmation of my love and acceptance and willingness to please him.

CHAPTER 20

A Maiden Voyage

"It's not where you travel that matters. Its who you travel with."

-Unknown

CALVIN AND I DECIDED TO take a much-needed trip as a way of 're-charging our batteries' after the wedding. Our destination was Puerto Rico as it was budget-friendly and required only a driver's license as documentation. The trip to Puerto Rico was significant in that it was a maiden voyage of sorts. It was for me, a kind of migration from one existential state to another from being merely an outsider living in America, to someone who had become a member of the community with family ties. I looked forward to exploring Puerto Rico, a US colony with Spanish antecedents and a Caribbean influence. I had seen pictures of San Juan, and its Spanish colonial architecture, that reminded me of old Port of Spain, the capital city of Trinidad and its colorful historic buildings around the Queen's Park Savannah.

I was very curious about how Calvin would react to the food. In a way, it was simply a reconfiguring of ingredients we used at home. The cuisine consisted of beans, rice, plantain, meat, cassava, and fish. The names of the dishes were different with perhaps some variation

137

in preparation and seasoning. I expected I would be able to recognize most of the ingredients. Suffice it to say that Calvin was not big on rice and beans such as the Arroz con Grandules or pigeon peas and rice. We call it Pelau at home. He could handle beans but the heavy carbs we Caribbean peoples were used to eating everyday was not a favorite of his. Cassava was completely foreign to him. He enjoyed the fried plantain dishes. I loved the way they prepared the fried plantain. It was 'mashed' together in a lasagna-like preparation called Pastelon. This preparation was different from the way we served it in Trinidad, where sweet ripe plantains are fried and served as a side dish.

He enjoyed the Pernil, which is a dish of slow roasted marinated pork. This dish is also a popular fare at Christmas for Trinidadians. He avoided certain types of seafood such as shrimp, clams, and crabs, while preferring the Red Snapper and Grouper dishes. It came as no surprised to me that the food was so similar, as we shared a common history, when Trinidad was under Spanish rule with slave populations.

I discovered that my husband is no different from the average American who has a penchant for sea bathing and the beach. Having grown up on an island, I can take it or leave it. I would rather comb the gift shops or look for unusual jewelry, preferably made by indigenous craftsmen. We were told that we should go to Loiza in the northern part of the island. There were some jewelry shops and cultural artifacts on display in their museum. On arrival, we found the history of this region to be compelling. Calvin willingly and without reservation loved to talk to the natives about their ancestry and their life in the village. We learned that in Loiza there once was a community of Tainos Indians whose chief was a woman named Loiza. I explained to him that the Tainos were indigenous to the Caribbean region as a whole and their population had been decimated through disease and ill treatment by the conquering Europeans.

We learned that in the 1600s, the indigenous population was joined by runaway slaves from the British colonies. Accordingly, there would be cultural and religious intermingling among the Tainos, Africans and Spaniards. Not surprising, Calvin wanted to know where he could see some of the indigenous musical instruments. There had been some unique developments which emerged in music and dance in the area that later spread throughout the country. I had no idea my husband was so interested in Ethnomusicology. He was in his element! He learned that the Bomba and the Plena, which now constituted the traditional folk dance of Puerto Rico, had originated in Loiza. The music and dance of the Bomba and Plena are unmistakably African, with rhythms emanating from barrel-shaped drums, maracas, tambourines, and jingles. Some of these percussion instruments were on display in the museum.

I also learned that Calvin had a tremendous interest in cultures. As a result of our curiosity, we learned that Loiza had the largest Black community on the island. We were told by people who resided in the town, about the Santiago Apostol festivities that usually took place in July. Some of the Vejigante masks and costumes were on display in a museum which, unfortunately was closed that day. Calvin insisted that we should return the next day to pay a second visit when we were sure they would be opened to visitors. I did not think that there would be anything worth seeing but I was mistaken. It turned out to be a trip well worth a return visit because Loiza's costumery was indeed unique.

I tried to determine the origin of the masks, but I could not fathom its source. I was certain they were not of West African origin, as they were made of dried coconuts with long spikes or horns in a halo-like formation, painted in bright colors. West African masks were generally made of wood, or as in Benin, copper, or ivory. I once read that 17th century Spaniards held processions in which Vejigante masks were used to represent demons. The costumes were made of flowing fabric in a jumpsuit fashion with extraordinary bat-like sleeves. There was a definite religious dimension to their festival/carnival, unlike our Trinidadian Carnival, which was a sort of tribute to Dionysius, the god of wine in Greek Mythology.

The next day we moved on from the traditional to the modern, and highly technological making our way to the Arecibo Observatory. The harrowing drive was an uphill climb on a narrow road with only one way in and out. We were able to take pictures of this amazing structure and to tour the visitors' center. In 1974 the 'Arecibo Message', in the form of radio waves, was beamed out to some 25,000 light years in the sky, as an attempt at creating an interstellar conversation with ET. The huge satellite dish lies in a crater surrounded by low lying hills. This imposing, technological, arthropod-like structure, is susceptible to the vagaries of the hurricane season, as Puerto Rico is situated in the hurricane belt.

From Arecibo, we decided to visit Ponce in the south. From the descriptions I had read, it seemed to be laid out in a design, similar to that Port of Spain in Trinidad. Since my husband had never visited my home, this would be a nice introduction. The cultural landscape of the plaza common throughout the Spanish realm was evident in downtown Ponce. The city was laid out in grid-like formation with north/south, east/west axes and at the point of intersection was the plaza, complete with fountains, benches, and a bandstand. The plaza, as the focal point of the community, was surrounded by the Catholic Church, city hall, and other government offices and private businesses. I was amazed by this cookie-cutter design which I later learned was typical in places once occupied by the Spaniards.

However, change was on the horizon. The plaza reflecting Spanish influences was gradually succumbing to the onslaught of 'Americanization'. Several of the older buildings had been converted into fast food restaurants such as Wendy's and Mc Donald, now clothed in Puerto Rican motifs. Once these had been family-owned shops with Spanish names. Now they were taken over by franchises and multinational corporations with English names such as City Bank and Gordon Jewelers.

Since it was a beautiful tropical day, we decided to walk and take some pictures. All around us the plaza struggled to maintain its integrity and historic appearance. The vibrant colors of the buildings reflected Spanish and Caribbean influences. As peoples of the Caribbean, our love for bright colors in architectural designs and intricate motifs had been inherited from the Spaniards. The Parque de Bombast building, erected in 1883, reflected Moorish/Spanish patterns with colors of rose pink, and grey. It once was a fire house. Behind it was the Catholic church, all white in stark contrast. Later we took a drive around the city and its environs, which were slowly succumbing to the effects of urbanization. There were the ubiquitous depressed neighborhoods, such as one may find anywhere in the Caribbean or in the US. While further out from the city center, there was always a 'La Alhambra', or upscale neighborhood with its ultra-modern homes, secured by its wrought iron and high concrete enclosure.

The following day was Thanksgiving. We were told that there was a group of natives who celebrated Thanksgiving in the rainforest. We decided to check it out. Shortly thereafter, we found ourselves in the company of men, women and children making an ascent to the top of a very steep hill. Many of the adults were older people who were in the habit of making this climb each year. No one I met spoke English. They spoke a dialect which was regional and foreign to me.

I struggled with communicating in my text-book Spanish. Who were these people, I wondered? Why would they choose to celebrate an American holiday at the top of a mountain? I considered that they were probably from the traditional Jibaro class of countryside people, or descendants of subsistence farmers, sharecroppers, and agricultural land tenants, who once made a living off the land.

Under American rule and capitalism, the Jibaro class is now part of the industrial machinery earning meager wages. They are now primarily landless. Today in Puerto Rico there is now a consciousness, a yearning to return to the era of pre-Americanism, when they were certain about their identity. Jibaro values and way of life now resonate among white-collar and blue-color workers, to the extent that the idea of the 'Puertorriqueno' or 'Puertorriquena' is synonymous with Jibaro culture and history. Many of the Jibaros in the early 20th century, and at the start of American colonialism, migrated from their mountainous homes to work in the urban areas. Standing atop this mountain, participating in this worship ceremony while surveying the land, was perhaps a way of evoking memories of the passage of time, when the Jibaro, a mountain people, had an impact on the political and economic life of the island.

The day after Thanksgiving we flew back to the US arriving in Philadelphia. As with many peoples and cultures I knew of, the Puerto Rican people struggle with their own dualism, of being betwixt and between two cultures, two languages, possessing an uncertain identity, and having a hankering for the past, as well as a skepticism about the future.

CHAPTER 21

It's Official

"My favorite thing about the United States? Lots of Americans, one America."

– Terri Guillemets

IN JANUARY 1998, THERE WAS a song - *The Boll Weevil Song*, written by Brook Benton. It haunted me for many days. The lyrics whirled and twirled in my mind.

Lookin' for a home.
Gotta have a home.
Searchin' for a home.
Lookin' for a home,
lookin' for a home,
A real hot home.
A real hot home.
Lookin' for a home,
A real hot home.

The daunting process of acquiring permanent residency was foremost on the agenda, with the plethora of forms needing to be completed. Deciphering 'legal speak' and having to navigate through the paperwork was essentially a rite of passage that was the fate of any immigrant who ventures into the realm of USCIS: United States Citizen and Immigration Services. This guarded and omnipotent agency was one that had the potential to wreck and ruin hope. While the Lady of Liberty is today subdued, she once, with outstretched arms, beckoned the homeless and displaced from Europe:

> "Give me your tired, your poor,
> Your huddled masses yearning to breathe free,
> The wretched refuse of your teeming shore
> Send these, the homeless, tempest-tossed, to me,
> I lift my lamp beside the golden door."
> -Emma Lazarus

To which I responded:
> *And so, they came in droves,*
> *From countries far and wide.*
> *With tongues Germanic and Romance,*
> *In speech and idiom pride,*
> *Led through the Golden door,*
> *Into a promised land.*
> *To rise and spread and thrive and grow,*
> *To breathe and to expand,*
> *And bar entry of the colored race*
> *Of indigent and hapless poor,*
> *Fanon's wretched of the earth.*

The process of acquiring a green card was the initial step towards naturalization and citizenship in the United States. My husband was required to start the process by filing an immigrant petition on my behalf. Once that was approved by USCIS, I then had to apply for an adjustment to my H1B status. Upon approval, I would be given an appointment for the data collection to be completed. This entailed getting fingerprinted and photographed to confirm my identity. The process would also entail the completion of a comprehensive background search. Success in this step of the process was also contingent on passing a medical exam by an approved USCIS doctor, to determine whether there is a history of a communicable disease such as syphilis, gonorrhea, tuberculosis, and leprosy. Questions relating to drug and alcohol abuse also feature prominently during the examination. At the end of the examination, the results would be given in a sealed envelope to take to USCIS at the interview stage.

The interview was conducted in downtown Pittsburgh. We took with us our marriage license, pay stubs, pictures, and other paraphernalia, that would support the case for residency and to prove that I was gainfully employed. Furthermore, we needed to establish that no marriage fraud was being committed and that we had been in a two-year long courtship. We were interviewed separately. Not surprisingly, the female USCIS officer was rude, impatient, and hostile, which I felt was almost a pre-requisite for the job. I had been warned about the stressful nature of these interviews. I did not think that there would be any problems since I had all the requisite supporting evidence to prove that my application was legitimate. Calvin and I were two intelligent, articulate people, who were employed and were not an encumbrance on the state. The habit of asking questions in a rapid-fire manner to ensnare and trap respondents seemed to be a familiar feature of determining legitimacy. What amazed me after all this time, is that I cannot recall most of the details of the interview except how unpleasant it was, and that I cried all the way home after leaving USCIS.

Change of status is like a rite of passage for immigrants seeking citizenship here in the US. It is a process that determines whether you are worthy to enter the body politic. It is also a course beset by obstacles. At the midpoint in my experience, the liminal, my thoughts were of change within myself. For me it meant that I was about to leave behind an aspect of myself and assume a different coherence. I wondered how it would affect me. What would this new identity mean? At this point I experienced heaven and hell. The anguish and uncertainty kept me up at nights. I feared the worst. For six months I lived in this state of purgatory, awaiting my Green card. Finally, it came in the mail. Even though I was eligible to apply for citizenship within three years, I had no desire to do so after that demoralizing, traumatic interview. I held onto the card for many years for fear of having to go through the same experience. I then sought legal advice about whether I should renew it when it expired. It was suggested that I should apply for citizenship immediately. I was warned that there was a chance the incoming Republican Government might not be pro-immigration. I was also informed that the process was a far more humane one with checks and balances in place and that there was recourse to complain.

While in possession of the Green Card, I was still a Trinidadian citizen and had to travel outside of the US on my Trinidadian passport. However, as a Green Card holder there was more flexibility in searching for employment opportunities. I could also vote in local and municipal elections though not Presidential ones. Then the era of the machine-readable passport arrived. I was not in possession of this document but was still travelling internationally on the old manual passport. Whenever I arrived in the US, I was not able to zip through the lines because I could not use the machine to gain entry. I discovered that Trinidad required a face-to-face interview in New York to apply for this passport. This would entail my being absent from work for a couple days, flying or driving to New York and staying at a hotel to be in New York for such an interview. I decided to try and obtain it when next I visited the island. On one such occasion, I took with me several documents such as birth certificate, my marriage license, Green Card, and affidavit of support. I was denied because I did not have an original copy of my divorce papers. Suffice it to say, I decided on my return, to apply for citizenship.

This time I had to pass an oral test about the history, organization, and Constitution of the United States. Again, I had a female interviewer, however, the interaction was cordial and easy going. Several weeks later there was the swearing-in ceremony in which I took a pledge of allegiance along with several other applicants. The oath of allegiance also involved renouncing my Trinidadian nationality, sadly. However, several countries among which are Trinidad and Tobago, Canada and the UK do not recognize the US oath of renunciation. These countries offer dual citizenship.

At its conclusion, the process from completing the citizenship application to the swearing- in ceremony, occurred in under four months. On the day I became a US citizen, I was able to apply for an American machine-readable passport. The process of becoming an American citizen was filled with anxiety and pain, but when it was all completed, I felt such relief that I could then rest my head at night without the fear of being separated from my husband. I was in a place where my husband was born, which he called home and for this reason above all others, there was no place where I would rather be.

CHAPTER 22

Putting Down Roots

*"Remember that not getting what you want is
sometimes a wonderful stroke of luck."*

~Dalai Lama

HOUSE HUNTING ON OUR OWN was proving more difficult than we
anticipated so we decided to get a realtor. Upon the recommendation
of a co-worker, we hired a woman whom we loved, the minute we
met with her. She was calm, confident, and reassuring throughout
the process. My husband, whose questions focused on design and
infrastructure, had his questions answered thoroughly and profes-
sionally. Perhaps due to a lack of experience, I concentrated primarily
on the cosmetic aspects of each property. Before any inspection of a
property, my husband insisted on first driving through the neighborhood, looking for red flags that hinted at potential instability of the
neighborhood, as evidenced by the number of properties for sale. If
it were the case that many houses were on the market, he explained
to me, it may indicate changes for the future regarding the property
value of our home.

Calvin's inspection always began with the roof, to determine the
age of the house. Once inside, he looked at floors, ceiling, and base-

ment. I felt that several of the properties we inspected, had our name on them. However, with his discerning eye, my husband would point out the flaws. Calmly and patiently, he would explain why we would not be buying a particular house. He would say, "No Gem, not this one the kitchen needs updating." Or, "No Gem, this house needs a paint job." That the owner did not make much home improvements over the years. For instance, he would simply state "look at the bathroom." Or, "We need more space between the next-door neighbor's house, since I like to practice at nights." This was to be an important factor in our decision to make an offer on a house.

This process went on for several months during which time we looked at a hundred houses. And then it happened! What would become our new house stood in a little community of homes, close to shopping and to the main highway. There was substantial space between the neighbors. The size was more than adequate. The kitchen was modern with a stone floor. The living and dining rooms had hardwood floors. I was beside myself with excitement, and I could not calm down. I truly saw myself living in this house. There was an inground pool at the back. The master bathroom was fairly modern. The house had a finished basement with office space and an extra bedroom. There was one full bathroom, two powder rooms, with a half bath off the master bedroom. Most importantly, the price was right. My husband loved it. I loved it. Marian our realtor said: "Ok, guys, then sell it to me! What do you like about it?" We both responded: "EVERYTHING!"

The closing proved to be more stressful than the actual year-long process of house hunting. Once we had the green light, my husband began the process of negotiating with the owner who was then residing in New York. The house had been on the market for a while which meant that he was probably paying two mortgages. Calvin, armed with the knowledge that the owner was probably a motivated seller, was determined to get the best price. The owner refused to budge on his asking figure. I was certain the sale would fall through and we would have to start all over again. At one point in the negotiation, they had reached an impasse when he gave the owner a twenty-four-hour moratorium to consider his final offer. I was sick with fear and anxiety while he was as cool as a cucumber:

> *"How can you be so calm? What if the seller refuses to budge?"*
> *"Then we will go with his offer. It doesn't hurt to try though."*
> *"I love this house and I hope we get it."*
> *"We will. Take it easy!"*

I was at my wits' end. I would have closed the deal long ago and accepted the seller's offer. I realized however, that my husband was an experienced negotiator. I knew something of his tenacity, but I did not know the extent to which he was prepared to go out on a limb. It was the first of many instances in which he taught me the art of bargaining while keeping my composure.

The next day the owner agreed to accept his offer. A week or so later, we had a call from him offering to give us back our hand money with extras if we would cancel the deal. He apparently had a new offer that came in after he had decided to sell to us. Calvin was very cordial in his response, explaining that it would not be possible to do so since his wife loved the house so very much.

Once we settled in, the next task was to furnish our new home. I soon realized that our tastes in furniture and interior design were different. They were polar opposites. The difference took on a North /South distinction. It was this difference of opinion around which we had our first disagreement. I preferred the 'South' style, with antique and intricate colonial design and motifs, somewhat light and fussy. I was drawn to the curving shapes, the shell-like motifs, the wing-backed chairs, and the rich, colorful, ornate fabric of the Queen Anne era. The Queen Anne's style of the eighteenth century remained popular in today's America. As I was a product of British colonialism, my attraction to an old metropolitan aesthetic reared its traditional head. Calvin, on the other hand, preferred the 'North' style - conservative, sturdy and predictable with muted tones. He also preferred cleaner lines, a less ostentatious style, with upholstery in a palette to match the neutral walls. He favored couches and loveseats that gave the impression of comfort and sturdiness, believing that the delicate nature and light wooden frames of antique furniture were sometimes uncomfortable and not always built to support much weight. We settled for a room-by-room design solution. I would pick out the furniture for the family room and dining room while he would concentrate on the living room and basement.

Landscaping was entirely my domain. I thought of creating a garden but soon realized that it involved more than I had bargained for, since I was unfamiliar with the types of flowering plants and shrubs that grew in this climate zone. I was more familiar with what is referred to here in the northern states, as annuals. In the Caribbean annuals grow all year round. Annuals are our perennials. Here in the temperate zone, the challenge was to select plants that could bloom at various stages, thus ensuring that my garden would have some color throughout most of the year. During the winter months, I would have to be content with the type of everyday perennials which bloomed for a short time in the Spring while the rest of the year the trees would be dull and ordinary. I took some comfort in the fact that they would provide some contrast to the winter colors.

I thought I should begin by taking an assessment of what I had to work with. There were several beds with rhododendrons and azaleas which were filled in with river rocks. I was not happy with the overall minimalist appearance of this monochromatic scheme of green foliage. I was determined to change the appearance of this lifeless garden-scape to reflect my Caribbean-ness and the tropical landscape I had left behind. Although it was late in the summer when we moved in, I decided to undertake the monumental task of removing the rocks and filling in the beds with chrysanthemums, marigolds, salvias, and coleus. I then added some hostas in the most shaded areas and New Guinea inpatients. I spent hours and resources in recreating my dream garden. Then it happened! Although I had made some inroads into my study of plants, I neglected to take into consideration the total environment and the role that animals and insects play in the overall balance of nature. I learned the hard way why the previous owner preferred rocks to flora. The challenge was with fauna for my garden became a veritable buffet for deer, groundhogs, aphids, mealybugs, and even wild turkeys.

CHAPTER 23

The Tree of Life

"You can have more than one home. You can carry your roots with you and decide where they grow."

- Henning Mankell

THE TRINITY OF ACCEPTANCE INTO a community: marriage, citizenship and homeownership precipitated more questions about how I thought of home and homeland. Where was the homeland for the foreign wife who is married to one of the locals? Was it the ancestral land of the husband or the ancestral land of the wife? Can there be two places that hold the same emotional attachment? Am I able to extend the roots which I have established in my homeland to that of my husband's?

It was around this time that I developed an interest in trees and logically, roots. We had quite a few trees on the property, prompting my curiosity about roots. I wondered what made it possible for a tree to withstand the forces of nature – such as strong winds and harsh dry conditions. I discovered that as a tree grows it establishes a rooting system which could be deep and wide, with depth for stability and width for survival. Even though the visible above-ground part of the tree appears to be permanently located in one spot, the part not visible, the part beneath the surface is anything but fixed. Roots are forever in a tireless quest coursing through and foraging the subterranean for water and nutrients. The root cap possesses an intelligence of its own which guides the root towards the source of nutrition. Some rooting structures extend way beyond the reach of the canopy. The wider the spread the better the chance for survival.

The symbolic Tree of Life, appearing in cultural legends across the globe with its roots extending in all directions represents unity and connection between the physical and spiritual realms. I began to embrace the Tree of Life as symbolic of my life's journey. It was a very appealing image, in that, metaphorically, its roots represented my roots, the roots of my ancestors, extending across continents and cultures, tracing the lines of my heritage. It was a lineage that extended back to Africa, India, to Trinidad and now here, in this place where I chose to nest. I surmise that because roots, by their very nature are constantly seeking out new sources for growth and survival, then rootedness in more than one culture should be enriching and revitalizing. Now I was establishing roots in a place that was not the ancestral homeland where my mother was buried, but it was in the place where my husband was born. As the roots spread out to include America, I wondered if it would affect my ardor for Trinidad? Was there a chance that with further acculturation, I would lose some of my Trini ways, aspects of myself, my Trini identity that distinguishes me from an American? Would there be a time when I would be so blended in as to be indistinguishable?

Without doubt, I have lost some of my indigenous mannerisms. I seem to be more reserved, less spontaneous. I am not as friendly and open as I used to be when I lived in Trinidad. I am more cautious, and less trusting. Living in America as a person of color does not guarantee me equal justice in the eyes of the law or equal protection thereof. Foresight or the ability to anticipate danger is always with me. It occurs to me that this is the reason Black parents socialize their children differently, especially with regards to safety and law enforcement. I have developed a heightened sense of clairvoyance, a premonition for danger. I worry constantly when my husband is gigging or travelling on the road at night. This sense of foreboding is one that I have developed while living in America. It has become so ingrained, that now I wear it like a cloak which I take everywhere, even when I visit Trinidad. While there, I prefer the main thoroughfare, and am wary of isolated areas. I seldom venture out alone.

I expect that the agent of change will over time mold and re-shape my identity as it does with all aspects of life. My appearance has changed such that friends I once knew when I was a native, do not recognize me when I see them. In fact, people I am introduced to when I am in Trinidad peg me at the onset as 'not from here' not local, even though I continue to speak with a strong Trini accent. Undoubtedly, many years of adapting to the language while living in the US have altered the way I speak, in order to be understood. Strangely enough, I experience a similar type of characterization when I meet people for the first time here in the US. My 'twang' immediately dubs me as foreign. Sometimes I feel like I exist in limbo - I am "not from here, not local" in the land of my birth, and foreign in the land where I now make my home.

As I think about my roots in the place where I was born, and where I now live, I am intrigued by a strange occurrence. I am recognized now as an American when I am in Trinidad and a Trinidadian when I am in America. I wonder about my status. Perhaps I am a Trinidad-American? For I am neither wholly one nor the other but both. But in what proportion? Am I half and half such as my 'Douglaness' or bi-racial ethnicity has labelled me in Trinidad? I have discovered that the longer the intervals between my visits to Trinidad, the further away I seem to move from 'Trinidad-ness.' Whenever I am in Trinidad, the fact that I visit so intermittently has made it difficult for me to slip easily into the vernacular, the native 'twang'. On the other hand, in America, because my accent distinguishes me as being foreign born, I could never be totally assimilated. There will forever be a disconnect between my Trinidadian and American selves. I think that this distance acts as a sort of counterbalancing influence to ensure that I know my place. Almost daily, I am reminded that I am a foreigner. I am often asked, "Which island are you from?" Or "How long have you been in the US?" Or "When was the last time you were home?" Or "You speak English very well."

There are marked changes in the way I see reality now, as a Trinidad-American. It used to be that I was totally consumed with the white aesthetic as the standard of beauty when I was a native Trinidadian. In those days, I thought in terms of binary opposites, that being in possession of a White or light complexion was preferable to being Black or dark. Every year the pre-carnival season would be heralded by the appearance in the media of young women who were vying for the opportunity to be crowned Ms. Trinidad and Tobago. I remember that looking at these young women, I did not see representations of myself. There were no Afro- or Indo-Trinidadian women with bi-racial features like me, blended in 'Douglarness' . These light and White winners would go on to represent the twin island nation in the Ms. Universe and Ms. World competitions.

For many years they were women with straight hair often blond and blue-eyed - just like the dolls we received at Christmas, year after year. As a child, the thought never occurred to me that dolls were made to represent other nationalities. The mere idea of a doll, was for me, a white doll. The anomaly of a black doll with curly hair did not make an appearance on the island until I was a grown woman. By then, I had internalized the white aesthetic. I wished for lighter skin and eyes the color of hazelnut. The man I once called husband often told me I was cute, but not beautiful. His niece, on the other hand, whose mother was an English woman and father half Portuguese, like himself was beautiful. His niece who favored her blond mother and had blue eyes.

I no longer defer to these notions of aesthetic beauty and grace. I am more knowledgeable of my history and of the imperialist culture that established those false standards of beauty. I no longer wish for what I once perceived as lushness of the greener grass on the other side, where I could not enter, with its rich harvest and fertile ground. Living in America, I am confronted each day by abundance and luxury amid poverty and degradation, among people of all colors. Instead, I now prefer to 'fertilize' and 'mulch' the arid side of the field I now occupy. I no longer fall prey to a singular notion of beauty that worships at the shrine of the alabastrine. From time to time, I glance at those opulent fields and I see loneliness, greed, and despair in the face of plenty. I see melancholy, suicide, and gloom. I have discovered that no one is exempt from mortality and that joy lies within, and not without. For life is fragile, finite, and profound, while beauty is skin deep and superficial.

The other binary to which I once adhered while living in Trinidad, and to some extent still do while living in America, is the male/female dichotomy in which the male is valued as naturally superior and the female as inferior. This set of values is an arduous road to travel, a pilgrimage beset by many obstacles, chief of which is a society in which patriarchy is prized. I grew up under its umbrella and am still over-shadowed by its reach. It is global and like a steamroller, its levelling action corrals women into an arena, thereby unencumbered to exercise its mastery. I sometimes capitulate and yield to conformity, having convinced myself that some battles are not worth the hassle.

Yes, Trinidad still harbors part of my roots. And since I visit infrequently, the lack of exposure and direct contact with my homeland obscures my roots. However, they are still alive and are still an integral part of who I am. Amazingly they are being sustained and kept alive because of the psychic and emotional stimulation of the root cap here where I now reside. I have surely left behind some of the less appealing ways of thinking such as coveting the white aesthetic. I now have an abiding sense of self, which I attribute to an exposure to many cultures. As wife, homeowner, and citizen, America has provided a vantage point, a scaffold from which I could look across the seascape and examine myself, and the place where I grew up. For this reason:

It was not for want of sustenance
I took leave of kindred spirits
To seek new ways of mastery
If perchance to cradle erudition
And to unfurl the jaundiced way
Of knowing.
To extend the reach of the island
The circumscribed
Inward looking, insular view
That I entered the metropolis.
For now, I have relinquished
Those icons I once held dear
Which then ambushed me into
Defeat and pessimism.
For with this new assurance
I wear the raiment of confidence
And esprit de corps.

CHAPTER 24

Carnival That Creole Bacchanal

"Yuh cyah vex when soca playin."

– Wayne Gerald Trotman

THE SOUND OF THE STEEL drums always draws me away from my current home and beckons me back to my homeland. The pulsating rhythms of the Tamboo Bamboo and the tassa drums lure me to my home where there is a lake of pitch. I am once again transported to a place where the national birds, the Scarlet Ibis and the Cocrico roost and nest, the wild Chaconia, the national flower, blooms every year in time to celebrate Independence Day in August. I miss the gaze of the 'Saga' boys who stand at the corner 'liming' (shooting the breeze) and I can almost feel Tanty's kiss on my cheek. I miss the bustle of Port of Spain around the Queens Park Savannah. I can all but taste the coconut water savored from the nut, or corn soup sipped from a Styrofoam cup, and oysters slurped from the shell accompanied by a hot sauce. The spirits of the ancestors are unsettled. I can feel it. They are beckoning me home where Trinidad-Tobago's culture with the music of Calypso, Soca, Chutney-Soca, Steelband and Tassa drumming, all blend together each year to produce the greatest bacchanal on earth in the Trinidad Carnival.

For my husband, it was to be his first visit to Trinidad. He had often expressed a wish to participate in the carnival, so we flew in on Wednesday before the carnival weekend. Where in the world is carnival as fantastic as that of Trinidad? 'Playing mas' takes place on Monday and Tuesday of carnival week. Thousands of masqueraders are organized into bands that are led by a king and queen. They dance, 'chippin' along the streets to the sounds of calypso and Soca, amplified by large speakers on 18-wheeler trucks.

More than anything else, Carnival is the one aspect of my home that I wish was possible to take with me and experience every year, wherever I live. On those occasions when I am in Trinidad at carnival time, as a spectator, I have found it difficult to stand still while observing the bands of masqueraders, for it is share torture simply to stand by without participating in the revelry. I want to jump in, throw my hands in the air, and dance to the rhythm of the music which is so infectious as to be narcotic. This is the one aspect of my homeland that I will never experience anywhere in the world. For the scintillating sound of the Steelband at Carnival is unique.

On this visit with my husband, I was determined to 'play mas' – to masquerade, dance in the streets and enjoy the festival. Up until the time when I left the island my involvement with Carnival was as a spectator while growing up. Later I chronicled carnival as a photographer with a small video production company. Trinidad Carnival is both history and pageantry. History is portrayed through that aspect of Carnival called Jouvay. It occurs in the wee hours Carnival Monday morning, heralding the beginning of the street parade. Jouvay represents an aspect of Carnival that developed after Emancipation when the ex-slaves were free to take part in the celebration. The freed slaves used the parade as a form of street theatre to highlight aspects of enslavement which were portrayed by small bands of revelers. Jouvay today, however, is reminiscent of both master and ex-slave depictions of the social dynamics of a past era. The celebrations begin at 2:00 am on Carnival Monday morning, with thousands of masqueraders parading in bands under different names, dressed in old clothing, smeared in mud, oil and talcum powder. The parade ends at mid-day on Monday and extends all day on Tuesday, by an aspect of Carnival commonly referred to as the 'pretty mass', which features the pageantry of the Carnival with its magnificent spectacle of glitz and glamour.

My husband and I decided on participating in the Jouvay celebrations. My sister arranged for us to join a band for the price of $250 US each, which would cover alcohol, all you could drink, mud, talcum powder, a snack and T-shirt with the band's logo. We were also afforded access to portable water from a truck to medical supplies, if needed, and portable toilets. A member's fee also included the ability to enjoy the event without fear of disruption, since most bands are equipped with security personnel who prevent nonmembers from gaining access. Modern-day Carnival is generally safe, having emerged from a period of violence among competing Steelband members. We met up with family, some of whom were seasoned players. My husband took to the oil, mud, and powder in good humor as he blended in with the natives 'chippin' away to the sounds of Calypso, Soca and Chutney-Soca. After five hours leading up to the break of dawn, the band finally dispersed at their headquarters.

While 'chipping' away along the avenue, in the wee hours of the morning, I thought of the ties that bind me to this place I call home. They are extraordinary, for I cannot experience Jouvay any other place in the world. While in the parade, I was overcome by a feeling of buoyancy and mirth brought on by the revelry of dancing in the streets to the sound of the Calypso beat. I began to entertain thoughts of postponing my return to the world of the American dream. The entire experience of Carnival provided an occasion for me to lay aside responsibility and be enclosed in a kaleidoscopic haze of glitz and glamour. This was the notion of home where I could relax and detach from all commitment.

A stone's throw from my sister's house, was the site of a fierce competition on steel. Later that day we headed out to the venue to observe a performance of seasonal music on steelpans. The young and the old as they banded together under such names as Harmonites Steel Orchestra, Melodian, Pan on The Move, and Arima All Stars. They played compositions on steel by Calypsonians – Sparrow, Shadow, and Singing Sandra. A Steelband orchestra in competition is a beautiful sight. With body movements synchronized to the beat, the band members on cue, after a long musical cadence, can sometimes, with aeronautical precision leap to the air in a state of euphoria. Without a break in the music, in a sweeping motion, the bodies of the men and women 'playing pan' would bend over and rise together slowly and deliberately, as to mimic the rising out of the ashes of the mythological bird, the Phoenix. For the history of pan music was shaded in controversy but was now finally an accepted art form internationally. And it was the brainchild of Trinbagonians.

Whenever I witness musicians 'playing pan', I cannot help but think of my early childhood. My mother would not allow us to visit a 'Pan yard' where the musicians practiced. Furthermore, she discouraged us from associating with 'Steelband men'. In those days it was a cultural art form in which young women were not allowed to participate, as it had been an art that grew out of those places that were considered 'depressed' and were associated with violence.

There was also another aspect of the Carnival, which for me, conjured mixed emotions. I was not always comfortable with the portrayal of women and the objectification of the female body that was a favorite topic from year to year among some Calypsonians. These portrayals perpetuated the stereotypes, both at home and abroad, of the Caribbean woman as loose, highly sexualized, and immoral. Like the Hottentot Venus of a century ago, a woman's bottom was often the prime target to be ridiculed by male calypsonians. The Calypso dance - the "jam and wine' gave men the liberty to gyrate their pelvic area against a woman's backside, while 'playing mas' during carnival. Women are often cautioned not to object, for fear of reprisal.

Nevertheless, I decided to take my husband to visit a Calypso tent which featured a lineup of the best in Calypso. Several hundred patrons stood at the entrance waiting to get in. The house band was reminiscent of his band in Pittsburgh with horns, guitars, percussion, and singers. Although he was 'hip' to the beat, the lyrics eluded him, especially the Calypsos based on themes concerning social and political intrigue. He was not altogether comfortable with creole and the vernacular and was further confused by the rapid-fire way Trinidadians speak. However, the language barrier did not deter him from enjoying the music and rhythms of Soca and Calypso. Music and instrumentation, he thoroughly understood even though this was a new beat. He listened in the quiet and absorbed way he was used to whenever we visited a jazz club to hear a band or a musician play. But he recognized that there was a unique aspect to the calypso tent.

I was relieved to see that the show had included several female Calypsonians who are now slowly debunking the stereotypical and extremely pejorative images of women. Today they are using the art form to focus on issues such as domestic violence, sexual harassment, motherhood, and empowerment. Furthermore, many Indio-Trinidadian women are using their own unique rhythms to shape a new genre in Calypso which is called Chutney-Soca.

Calypso, like Jazz is also a diasporic music, developed on the periphery, and among the poor. My husband had a fresh perspective on the role of the Calypsonian. He thought of Calypso as a musical type of speech, or genre. I had not thought of Calypso in this way. To his ear, the Calypsonian was like an orator who delivers his 'speech' to a captive audience, whose response to a good paunch line can illicit thundering applause and infectious laughter. While the Calypso lyrics could convey criticism, there was often an element of hope and humor, to dispel feelings of doom and gloom. A good Calypsonian knows how to use witticism, double entendre, and irony to turn his diatribe around. After all, people frequented the tent to relax and have fun.

My return home to the land of my birth, on this occasion with my husband was revealing. I was married and had become a US citizen and was settled in the country where he was born. His family I now considered my extended family. I had often felt that it was possible that I could experience a conflicting sense of loyalty for one homeland above the other. But this trip proved otherwise. I was discovering that living in Trinidad was so unlike that of living in America that contact with each culture gave rise to its own unique way of participating in this world. Over the years, I had experienced many changes in identity, from a British colonial to a Trinidadian and now a Trinidad-American, all of which tended to enhance my world view.

At an early age, I was identified as 'Dougla' – a person of no particular ethnicity, being neither African nor Indian, but both. It was a time when the people of Trinidad-Tobago thought of their identity as either that of the children of Mother India or of Mother Africa. We the children of the 'Dougla' caste, had no unique claim to a particular heritage, until the island became independent. It was the occasion when the founder of the nation rebuked and exhorted us to consider nationhood. This would mean that we would need to relegate racial differences to the background, shed the cloak of the exile and don the garments of citizenry, to be a collective of people, one nation, one state. Still at times, we continued to entertain romanticized memories of our great-grandparents and the lure to return to the ways of our old Motherland. As a result, beneath the surface today, there exists surreptitiously, a hint of divisiveness and disunity among Trinbagonians. Fortunately, this is kept at bay by the force of an emergent culture, representing the Indio and Afro traditions. At times, the impact of this culture is such that it functions as an alloy of such adamantine strength, as to be able to bring the two races together.

There is an aspect of the land of my birth I would like to insert into America society. It is the way in which we, of this multicultural nation have been able to co-exist. Perhaps Trinbagonians have arrived at a solution to reduce racial tension. I believe it has to do with the value we place on Carnival as a means of bringing us together, not for a week but throughout the year, to produce a spectacle that all can be proud of. Trinidad Carnival is at once an artistic endeavor but also a uniting force. While the potential for social unrest and violence between the two dominant groups is always present, Trinidad has managed to escape the bloodshed of Guyana, a country with a similar ethnic composition.

Once upon a time, Trinidad was named by the historical seafarer and pilferer, Christopher Columbus, to represent the Holy Trinity of his religion. Today, a different trinity holds us enthralled and as one - that of Carnival, Calypso and Steelband. Apart from the festival which takes place once a year, the preparations are all consuming as to occupy us all year round. Since so much time and effort are devoted to carnival and masquerade, Trinidadians are said to be hedonistic, that they live for pleasure and enjoyment, that we love a good fete, and are self-indulgent. While that may indeed be true, we are credited as being the most amiable and approachable of all Caribbean peoples. Perhaps this can be attributed to the blending of two disparate cultures which upholds the trinity of Carnival, Calypso and Steelband. One thing I can attest to, is that the annual tradition of Carnival confirms that cross-cultural contact can be creatively successful. A direct result of this process is the emergence of Chutney-Soca, which is the unification of the Indian musical genre with Afro-centric Calypso rhythms. For Carnival provides a space to come together where social barriers are broken down and where the 'all-ah-we-is-one' ideology prevails. At Carnival time, King Carnival reigns absolute in a land where we can laugh at each other's foibles. The parade on Carnival days as street theatre, provides freedom to mimic and mask our infirmities as a nation.

CHAPTER 25

Self-Discovery

THE OCCASION OF VISITING THE land of my birth together with my husband was revealing in many ways. Never was I so aware that I was a woman existing in two cultures and two worlds. Take for instance, dancing. The music I grew up with has so shaped my rhythm, that whenever I have the urge to dance, my steps always seem to be a variation of the 'chipping' along movements of the calypso beat. On many occasions, in America, when I am out dancing with friends at a disco or R&B concert or even Rock concert, I seem to experience the beat differently, so that I am often out of step with the rest of the dancers. I also seem to be living this duality in other ways as well such as through my sense of taste. Here in America, for instance, whenever I cook, I tend to mix and blend herbs and seasonings which are not unique to Caribbean dishes, in such a way as to create a distinctly Caribbean flavor. In some mysterious way, I seem to be guided by the need to revive the memory of my Caribbean tastebuds. Could it be that some indelible and lasting impression is guiding my hand and directing the correct measure of herbs and spices to use to create a distinctly Caribbean flavor? And is this the experience of other foreigners who miraculously recreate flavors, reminiscent of their homeland out of commonplace ingredients?

My return home on this occasion of Carnival, also happened to be a revelation of the self - a kind of peeling, layer by layer, to take a serious look at the world in which I grew up. The presence of my husband on this visit proved to be an integral part of this process of self-discovery. He was also eager to learn everything about my world, and to that end I assumed the role of guide and educator. As a result, this trip would not be the usual return visit when I would hang loose and unwind in a delightful haze of paradise - just enjoying the sun, sand, and sea. For in the past, whenever I visited, I refused to examine the hard truths, the consequences of crime and drugs reaping havoc on my people, and the health hazard posed by the fast-food franchises, such as Wendy's, McDonald's, Popeye's, Taco Bell, KFC, and Burger King. In my role as guide and informer, this trip with Calvin coincided with the unveiling of self and circumstance.

My husband had heard of the fantastic Trinidadian cuisine. He was anxious to sample the local dishes – the bake and shark, the pelau, the delicious callaloo, black pudding, oil-down, or roti. Much to his chagrin, he discovered that local foods were not franchised but were available here and there through small mom and pop shops. We had to drive twenty miles to the seaside town of Maracas in the Northern mountainous area to get a bake and shark and forty miles to Debe in the center of the island to get some Saheena and Baiganee. "But American fast food was at every street corner. How does one account for that?" he asked. "I guess the white gaze was still looking over our shoulder dictating what our lifestyle should be; what we should eat and wear, and our moral and spiritual values." I replied. This was also true of the grocery stores which were replicas of the ones in every town and city in America. When did we develop a taste for hotdogs and hamburgers, French-fries, pizza, and Starbucks coffee? Our local handcrafted jewelry made from leather and indigenous materials such as shells and seeds were not easily available. However, the variety made in

China, big and brassy and commonplace were plentiful. "How about a trip to Bucco Reef on the sister island of Tobago?" I asked:

Where we mutilate the coral
Ripping apart the tentacles
To peddle the branches.
And crush the young polyps
With crepe-soled feet
As we trample through
the fragile outgrowth
To Attract the tourist.
Where our waste, unrestrained
Seep into the delicate balance
Of the coral world
Poisoning the plankton.

Suffice it to say we never did make that trip to Bucco for we were told most of the reef was destroyed.

Up to this point, Calvin had met few Trinidadians. He had visited many of the other Caribbean islands over the years but not Trinidad. My sister and her husband were our hosts. My dad was still alive, so Calvin was eager to meet him and the rest of my family. My younger sister had been to our wedding, so he had met her and since arriving had struck up a bond with her husband. I took him to my father's house where they spent several hours in conversation talking about this and that, about work, politics, and Trinidad. As I listened to my father, I was overcome by a deep sadness. I felt a bleakness that was marked by isolation and pathos. I looked around the room and the one solitary picture on the wall was that of a poem by Anonymous about friendship - 'Friendship is a golden chain/ that binds two friends together/ and if you do not break that link/we will be friends forever.'

After our visit, my husband was surprised that there were no pictures of family - of children being christened, taking their first steps, outside at play on a sunny day, enjoying a day at the beach. There were no pictures of birthday celebrations, decorating the Christmas tree, or children opening their Christmas presents. There were no portraits of my mother, my grandparents, or great-grandparents. Looking around the room, there was nothing - no record, no memorabilia, no certificates of achievement. "Were there picture albums?" he asked. "Why were there no memories?" he enquired. I had never thought of it. Once Calvin raised the question I had no choice but to re-examine my childhood upbringing.

For as far back as I could remember, I had always felt the veil, the mask, the curtain drawn to disguise the brick wall between my parents. While growing up, I had come to accept without reservation, the enigmatic relationship between my parents. My mother wanted more out of life, though she had no marketable skills. My father was 'a jack of all trades and master of none'. He struggled to provide for his family, while at the same time was crushed by limited opportunity and a lack of appreciation for his effort. My parents' union was forged out of the fires of discontent and bitterness. They were two people trapped in the doldrums of adversity and united by misfortune and poverty. As I thought about the lack of photos and mementoes, it occurred to me that photos represented a sentimental journey. Photo albums were archives of pleasure and joy to reminisce with family and friends when the need arose. But what about a life's journey that has been exhausting, laden with problems and strife? Why would one want to document and remember with photos, lives that were fraught with hardship and sadness?

I never spoke to my father about his relationship with my mother and the cause of their unhappiness, nor about the estrangement of his family. Moreover, I have never gotten the full story of my mother about her upbringing. I so wish I had. I lament the fact that I did not press her to talk about her early life. As a child growing up, it was 'grown people's business-don't-ask questions.' After I left my parent's house, as a young woman while living in Trinidad, it took me several years to re-examine the bitterness I harbored for my father. Daily, while growing up, I was acutely aware of the animus of my mother towards my father. Her portrayal of him was not one of which to be proud. If there is one redeeming aspect of my marriage to my first husband, for which I am grateful, it was his suggestion that I should reconsider my relationship with my father. He wanted me to recall the fact that my father never deserted the family. As a result, after giving it much thought, my father and I developed a closer bond in the years that followed, though he was still reticent about family matters, claiming, "Mother is not easy." My sister's children became the essence of his later life, especially his granddaughter.

I once did a DNA test to determine my ancestry. It revealed a mapping profile of 49.5% as being connected to Central and South Asia on my mother's side and 48.5% from Sub Saharan West Africa on my father's. There was a 2% identification with a prehistoric human species that disappeared 40,000 years ago. In Trinidad, I am a 'Dougla' woman. I stand at the imaginary confluence of where the rivers Ganges and Nile meet. The blood of two nations, flows through me. I am entrusted with the knowledge of two traditions, two cultures. My 'Dougla-ness' strives for unity for I can never elevate one aspect of my heritage by denigrating the other. Therein lies the duality of which I am constantly aware.

Growing up in a multiracial home presented some unique challenges. Both my parents were born on the island, as were their parents. The tri-color structure of the Trinidadian colonial society with whites at the top, mulatto and lightly complected in the middle, and Afro and Indo Trinidadians at the bottom, was the inherent social structure for many years, up to and after independence. Under colonialism, the white gaze of the master's disapproving eye, together with the grand design of divide and rule, defined a way of controlling the masses. It ensured that the Indians and Blacks were forever kept apart. This was further exacerbated by stereotypical images perpetuated by each group for the other which tended to look with disfavor at inter-racial marriages.

When an Indian woman married a black man, it was generally looked upon with disfavor by her family members. She was also not fully accepted by his family. I remember my mother once took it upon herself to contact her estranged brother whom she had not seen since they were children. I was about ten at the time. He was not very friendly and seemed unwilling to develop a relationship. He was married to an Indian woman and had Indian children. Both my grandmothers and great-grandmothers were not present at our birth but came to know us later while growing up. My father's family paid the occasional visit, but it was obvious that they were not keen on my mother. We lived a more-or-less isolated life which in time became increasingly isolated as the older generation passed away in time.

My sister Janet, who is a year younger than I, was my mother's favorite child. She was the anointed, the chosen one, the closest to my mother, with blue ribbon status, the best-liked of the three daughters. Her quiet temperament and generous nature singled her out to be the sacrificial lamb. As the exalted, she was my mother's confidante, privy to the source of her affliction and her tortured soul. My sister wore this responsibility like an albatross around her neck. For many years she wrestled with anxiety and unease, bordering on depression. She convinced herself that she was responsible for my mother's happiness. Fearful of being seen as ungrateful, she stayed in the nest way into adulthood. Then one day she flew the coop, fatigued, and exhausted by the demands of self-sacrifice. I was already in a serious relationship, having left home but making frequent visits.

Both my sister and I dated men from opposing ends of the race spectrum; she gravitated towards Indo, and I towards Afro. Occasionally, I dated men who were referred to as Trinidad white. Whenever my sister's Indian boyfriend would take her to visit his parents, she was not always welcomed, for she was not 'pure Indian' but a 'mixed breed Dougla-girl', of whom they disapproved. Often in my sister's presence, the older folks would try to discourage the relationship by letting her know what their feelings were towards mixed marriages. Sometimes, in her presence they would malign her in Hindi, so much so that after several attempts, she gave up that pursuit and settled on a foreigner - a British expat living in Trinidad.

This journey home continued to be challenging, as I was confronted by so many issues I had never before considered. Never was the need to examine cultural memory and social landscape so very pressing. Now it was essential to undertake this task. I attributed this sense of urgency, to my husband's presence on the island, which offered a new lens, to examine aspects of my family which were so familiar to me as to be invisible. Was the homeland I hungered for an actual reality? Did it ever exist? How much of it was contrived and invented? What was the effect of migration on the validation of my past existence? It appeared to me that over the years while living in America, I had developed a longing for the sanctuary of my homeland, which I had imagined as an arcadian world where I believed life was picturesque and unspoiled. In my mind, Trinidad had come to represent paradise, a place to escape to when survival in the metropolis felt like an attack on my sanity. It was a place of refuge, an asylum to recover and restore myself.

While living in America, I was able to maintain this image of an idyllic world by not reading the Trinidad Guardian online, or glossing over negative reports on social media. I now realize it was a deliberate conscious attempt at maintaining this fantasy. This visit, however, imposed new responsibilities upon me as a tour guide, thereby forcing me to put aside illusion and confront reality. For the first time since leaving, I was forced to listen to the voice of my people through the media, and I discovered that the problems of day-to-day existence were the same as in America. Trinidad was not the sanctuary I envisioned, but a place beset by first-world afflictions: drug addiction, money laundering, political intrigue, unemployment, and poverty. It was a modern-day society, where ambition and guile directed the competition for limited resources.

Now the notion of home as being a paradise, and my childhood as idyllic, had to be discarded if I were to remain true to myself. It was a chastening experience. I began to reassess my memory of homeland as sanctuary, and of a place fixed in time and changeless. I realized that culture was not static or gridlocked within an era long gone. Frankly, with each return I recognized less and less of the landscape. The transformation in some villages was stark. The shift out of the past was radical. For instance, where was the old El Dorado where I grew up? Were it not for the street signs I would lose my bearings! There have been times on previous visits when I did not meet a single acquaintance from my past. Even the vernacular was undergoing change. During casual conversation among the young people, new expressions and idioms in the language have kept me guessing what the conversation was about. During this visit, homeland seemed now to be a myth, no longer relevant in the psychic and spiritual corners of my mind. I thought of a word for breaking out of this condition – 'Mindscaping!'

Nevertheless, there is a spiritual quality of the land that keeps me captive regardless of changes. I cannot explain it. It is what animals experience - a sort of innate attraction, a homing quality associated with their birthplace that keeps pulling them back. This same connection to home was responsible for the euphoria I always felt on arrival - a sort of rapture. What is it? This urge to enfold my arms around the green mantle of her mountainous peaks, to kiss the cheeks of the fresh morning dew and to sing to the sunrise. At times I often cried at the setting sun at day's end as it descended into the horizon. What is this force that pulls me back, time and time again? Maybe it is connected to a certain vitality that we acquired when in early childhood, we first step on the land. With those tentative first steps we may have received - a sort of imprinting.

CHAPTER 26

Fragments of a Dream

"All the honor and the glory/Alma Mater shall be thine."

-Cheyney University Alma Mater

WE HAD BEEN MARRIED JUST three years when I received an exciting job offer. While time was not exactly opportune for such a potentially disruptive change, it was one that I had to consider seriously. I felt I was at the crossroads in choosing one path over the other. But my journey through life must continue. Progress can often hinge on a break in routine. There was an opportunity to direct an Office of Admissions at another State University. This time it was at a Historically Black College in eastern Pennsylvania. We lived in western Pennsylvania, 500 miles away. Accepting the job would mean that I would need to find an apartment and commute on weekends. It would mean an advancement for my career which I considered to be wise and prudent. My husband could take early retirement and concentrate on performance and honing his musical skills. Calvin wondered if I was fixed on the idea. I convinced him that I was. He suggested that I should take up an instrument. "It would help to breach the distance." I decided on the flute.

The voice of judgement from my friends, my African American friends, in particular, was of a vociferous, "NO!" There was not a single word of affirmation. There was no applause or commendation, no well-wishes - just a sinister note of impending gloom and disappointment. The position had been vacant for some time, and enrollment had been on a steep decline for a number of years. In addition, there were some fiscal problems.

Undaunted, and perhaps more curious than ever, Calvin and I made a trip to look the campus over. Cheyney University is a member of the State System of Higher Education of fourteen universities. I had been on the campus several times to attend State System recruitment efforts hosted by Cheyney. During these events, guidance counselors from the Philadelphia School District were in attendance. All fourteen institutions host these programs as a recruitment effort to bring guidance counselors together in a college fair setting on the various campuses. I had not seen the entire campus, but I had a vague idea of the layout. I was beside myself with excitement as we approached the historic seed of the campus, where it all began. The quad was encircled by magnificent stone buildings which disappointingly were closed to the public in a state of disrepair. Apparently, monies were due to the University by the state of Pennsylvania leading to years of underfunding of the school. The result of which was a shortfall for academic programs, recruitment, and repair of the infrastructure.

As I stood in the center of the quad, I felt the ill-will of my friends towards the school slowly being replaced by an overwhelming obligation to this Cheyney University, which some say is the oldest institution of higher learning in the US. As an educator, I knew the history of the struggle to bring education to African American boys and girls from as early as the eighteenth century. I had read of the history and success of the Institute of Colored Youth (ICY) in

Philadelphia, the forerunner to Cheyney University. Fanny Jackson Coppin, the first female Principal of ICY, I held in the highest esteem. I had read her autobiography and I thought that maybe her hard work in increasing the enrollment of ICY and extending its curriculum could have been one of the reasons why it became necessary to expand on the school's infrastructure. Even though she had retired before ICY moved to its Cheyney Farm location, twenty-five miles west of Philadelphia, and was later renamed Cheyney State Normal School, I considered her an integral part of Cheyney's history.

On our way back to Pittsburgh, after the visit, I reflected upon the disparity and unfairness of the funding structure being based solely upon enrollment, and the dilemma that ensued. Regardless of this problem my mind was made up. The following week I headed back to begin work. I would live in Media, Pennsylvania. I even located a flute teacher who lived in the area.

Cheyney University of Pennsylvania was founded by Richard Humphreys (1750-1832) born in the West Indies, on the island of Tortola. The name Tortola means 'turtle dove' in Spanish. Does that make him a Caribbean or a West Indian? Was this a sort of serendipitous call from the past? Was there a metaphoric hand, a rip in the surface of time, reaching out to a fellow West Indian, a Caribbean born to take up the mantle?

I had no problem responding to the call for it had become second nature to me. My work with students of color on a predominantly White campus before had resulted in a strong sense of commitment. So important was this experience, that I was sure I had found relevance and purpose in my life. In those early years, I had become an 'evangelist' for education among African American students. Slowly this commitment resulted in a parallel pursuit for the meaning of 'home' and an inquiry as to whether I could experience 'home' in more than one place. No doubt, had I not found meaning in my work and my connection with my students, I would have returned to Trinidad. Furthermore, my marriage to Calvin was another reason for making America my home. Now with the acceptance of this job, I considered it an affirmation that I was indeed 'home' and that along with this recognition, I could not refuse to give of my services.

I suppose that there are other ways in garnering support when it is not forthcoming from one's circle of friends. I found it in a most unconventional place. I chose to tap into the life history of both Richard Humphreys and Fanny Jackson Coppin. At the same time, I had discovered the works of Carl Jung, the famous Swiss psychiatrist, and psychoanalyst who wrote extensively about the reinforcing quality of latent memories, which are hardly discernible. He considered that the experiences of the entire human race are stored and embedded in our "collective unconscious mind" and can be tapped into on occasions. If we could identify certain touchstone in our common experiences with our fellow humans - past, and present, we could make use of the wisdom and life lessons of previous generations to guide us into action. This idea resonated so strongly with me that I embarked on a mission to discover the essence and life's purpose of both Richard Humphreys and Fanny Jackson Coppin, which I could use as a beacon to lead me through this leg of my journey.

I found that Richard Humphreys, the founder of Cheyney University, and I shared a few things in common. As people of the tropical garden of the Caribbean, we both had lived a life under imperialism, experienced migration to a foreign land, and had undergone a period of acculturation. For different reasons, we both had an invested interest in the education of young African American men and women. Fanny Jackson Coppin's appeal to me was her conviction about the redemptive power of education as a step forward. She was a woman who was once a slave, but through education became a pioneer. I found that I had been adopting her mantra unconsciously all those years during my recruitment days while on the road from city to city, to inform young men and women, on what was possible.

It was an astonishing coincidence that this man and woman who were alive during the eighteenth and nineteenth centuries, would be tied to this place, this institution, at which I was offered an opportunity to work. I could feel their hands extending towards me across the centuries in anticipation, so that I would take up the challenge. Here were two people, whom I had never met, both related to the same cause, awakening a desire within me to return a favor to the African American community. I once mentioned to my previous boss that one day I would find a way to repay all he had done for me, as well as his confidence in my ability. I saw this as the occasion to return the favor: one which would entail working at a Historically Black Institution of Higher Learning. I felt I was the missing side of the triangle, the third leg. I am often reminded of a certain property of a triangle, that if you were to exert pressure on any of its sides, it tends to be absorbed evenly throughout the rest of the structure, to the extent that it becomes difficult to break. I began to feel fortified into action and I felt that there was some quality in me that could be harnessed to boost the enrollment. So absorbed was I in finding the essence of Cheyney's founder, Richard Humphreys that a few days before I arrived on campus, he came to me in a dream.

His voice was as lucid and penetrating as if he were sitting beside me:

"You must know Tortola is the largest of the British Virgin Islands with a colorful history of piracy. I was born there in 1750. It once was the permanent home of Captain Kidd. Under British rule, white settlers

from as early as the fifteenth century established a plantation colony on the island.

"The lure was sugarcane which was fueled by African slaves. My parents were British, second-generation plantation owners. My family owned slaves. In the early days when sugar was king my parents did fairly well. By the turn of the century, Tortolian society was beginning to feel the effects of a call to dismantle the slave trade. Several Quaker families on the island such as the family of John Lettsom and William Thornton freed their slaves long before Emancipation.

"My parents were Quakers. While the few Quaker slave masters in Tortola were more humane, in the way we treated our slaves, there were many instances of atrocity, metered out to the men and women in bondage. There were incidents of slaves losing their limbs while trying to escape, of the disfiguring and the branding and floggings, of the separation of families during inter island commerce, and of rape and miscegenation. It was all there, on a smaller scale, nevertheless insidious. I would say that as a young lad that this was probably the beginning of a unique sensibility on my part to the plight of the Black race. I hated slavery. My playmates were the children of our house slaves. My best friend Mathew, born the same year, was a Negro slave who shared my books and sometimes my clothes. He was more of a sibling to me than Thomas, my own brother.

"In 1764, I was told that the time was ripe for me to take up a trade. I was fourteen. Arrangements were made for me to be apprenticed to a goldsmith in Philadelphia. The journey from my tropical garden home to Philadelphia would take seventeen days by steamer. I was leaving home and all that I held dear to me- my friends and my island. I was leaving the place where my umbilical cord was buried, that part of earth where I took my first steps. I would miss those rugged hills where I cascaded down on a makeshift slide of coconut branches.

"My head swam with many questions. Would I be able to make a home in America where the buffalo once roamed, and the deer and the antelope were slain for sport? The lyrics of a song, "Home on the Range" kept replaying in my head throughout the voyage despite the fact that all was not as bucolic as the song declared, at least as far as Black people were concerned. The buffalo was extinct, and the antelope and deer were shadowy figures. It was surely a place where all that was heard was a 'discouraging word.' And 'where the skies were cloudy all day' because the home on the range was beset by an evil presence of men in bondage. The sensation of embarking felt like slipping out of the womb and landing in a sea of foreboding and danger. There were long nights I shared with the stars and the sleepless sea as company.

"At the age of fourteen I believed as a member of the Society of Friends, as a Quaker, that all persons were to be valued. It was my credo. In Philadelphia where I was to be apprenticed for seven years as a gold/silversmith, I was beset by longing for my home, my island of the Turtle Dove, of peace and harmony. For here where I found myself there was none. Protest was the order of the day, of daily disturbances in response to the Sugar Act, the Quartering Act, and the Stamp Act. The American colony was in turmoil in 1764. There was acrimonious conflict with the Crown about taxation without representation. A few years later we would suffer the Boston massacre. I lament the fact that this was not remotely close to a Tortolian tropical haven.

"Now living in America among Orthodox Quakers, I came into contact with slaves escaping from the South via the Underground Railroad, which was neither a railroad nor underground but a network of secret trails and houses to enable safe passage from the southern states to the north. I was privy to the barbarity and nefarious accounts of slave masters. Slowly but surely, I was resolved that one day when I could, I would do something to help my fellow man.

185

"I had heard of Anthony Benezet, one of the earliest abolitionists, who in 1750, the year of my birth on Tortola, had set up a night school for slaves at the Quaker School where he taught. I thought that maybe I could establish a school for the children of the people of the African continent. Twenty years later in 1770, I knew Benezet had founded another school for Black children in Philadelphia. Furthermore, he bequeathed a portion of his estate which was to be used after his wife's death, to further educate the children of African descent, Mulatto and Native American. Anthony Benezet's ideas for education as a means of empowerment left an indelible mark on me. It was the beacon in my quest to help the damned and despaired. I believed that education and learning a trade would be commensurate with personal success and serviceability to society.

"For many years I followed the struggle of the freed men and women to compete for employment with other ethnic groups such as the Irish and other Europeans. I followed the accounts of the struggle by Negro boys and girls to get educated. I read of the attacks on homemade attempts to set up private schools and of the torching of buildings where there were attempts to educate the Negro. We Quakers, in the 1770s had made some inroads to educate Black children. The African Free Schools established by the Manumission Society were not about training and education, but about catechizing. These schools did nothing to train the freed man. What was needed were trade schools and schools to train teachers. I had set up some small endowments here and there, and scholarships to Oberlin for the education of Black boys and girls. After a successful career as a silversmith, I was in a better position to make a move towards setting up an institution for colored children. In the winter of 1828, I had taken a bad fall which set me back for almost a year. I was barely mobile, and my dreams were pushed to the background.

"Now, in those days there was an influx to the Northern States of slaves and ex-slaves. This migration set the stage for an acute hostility, racism and

competition for jobs and housing. One result was the bloody Cincinnati Race Riots of 1829. I had heard how recently arrived ethnic groups from Europe were given citizenship and were favored for employment. That the freed man and woman who were born here in America had to step back because they were Black. That they had no representation in the branches of government even though they were taxpayers. What irony! Because these United States were founded because of just such a cause. I thought what perversity this is! We were doing to others what we would not have done to ourselves. The Golden Rule was a mockery. I was now an old man. In those declining years I seemed more determined than before to flout the prevailing sentiment. From whence came this courage to educate the Negro? It came from man's inhumanity. I knew it was an unpopular cause but I already had one foot in the grave. I would dare for I had no time to waste.

"For years I knew the path towards education was the only way out of servitude. We Quakers during the eighteenth century had already founded several schools for the descendants of the slaves. So, the idea of a school was not new to me. Ultimately it was the Race Riots in 1829 that prompted me into changing my will. My mind was made up. My instructions in 1832 to my executors, were to erect an institution to instruct the descendants of the African race in school learning, in branches of the mechanical Arts, trades, and Agriculture and in teaching. At the age of 79, I had amassed a small fortune as a gold/silversmith and had decided to bequeath ten thousand dollars towards the founding of the Institute for Colored Youth (ICY) in Philadelphia."

Richard Humphreys, founder of ICY which later became Cheyney University of Pennsylvania died before his dreams were realized. I was intrigued by this West Indian immigrant to the United States. This seemingly unassuming man, at the age of 79 had changed his will to make provisions for a school to educate Black boys and girls. Correcting for inflation, this would amount to a quarter million dollars in today's currency. It was then one tenth of his wealth. These were turbulent times. Education for Blacks was unpopular. Attempts by people of good will to educate Black boys and girls were met with violence. For example, in 1838, Pennsylvania Hall was torched during a meeting of Quakers to discuss education for the ex-slaves. Humphreys was not simply courageous and committed, he had tremendous foresight in determining the needs of African Americans once slavery was abolished. He envisaged a need for Black leaders and teachers, a vision that was to be the genesis for a school which could train students in all aspects of education.

There were other small legacies and endowments. Today the Humphreys Foundation still manages a scholarship fund for African American students. Unfortunately, he did not live to see the opening of the Institute in 1837. In 1832, the year of his death, was to witness the continued development of a strong sentiment favoring the colonization of Blacks-back-to Africa, notwithstanding the fact, that most African Americans had never seen Africa and were born in America. The movement was favored mainly by Whites especially Southern slaveowners. There was some interest among the abolitionists in the movement. However, it was unlikely that Richard Humphreys would have seen the merits of such a solution since he chose to direct resources towards education rather than emigration.

I imagined what those early discussions concerning the execution of his will must have been like in the Board Room of the trustees selected by Humphreys. They were all elderly contemporaries within his circle and all White men. I imagined if I were to read an account of the early stages in the setting up of the institute, it would probably describe the many challenges in the following way:-

On February 25,1837, we, the Managers who were chosen by Richard Humphreys to carry out his plans to set up the school, began the discussion and reviewed the options. We had decided on the popular Manual Labor program that was introduced by Oneida College near Utica in New York. It was to take the form of a farm school which would teach students the principles of Agriculture along with academic subjects.

In 1839 we bought a farm in Bristol township, seven miles outside Philadelphia. The name African Institute was first considered but we soon rejected the idea, finally settling on The Institute for Colored Youth, ICY. We, the thirteen Quakers would be the managers. There were fourteen boys enrolled in the program. We settled on White teachers. Students would be engaged in hard labor and studies in a ten-hour workday. As the years went by, we noticed a decline in the number of students enrolled. Many of them ran away. Within eleven years the program was in serious trouble. We had to do something, so we decided to reexamine the direction for the school, and in the end, we settled upon the teacher training aspect of Humphrey's wishes.

In retrospect, hindsight is forever a good lens through which to in-form future planning. We examined schools where manual labor was the main emphasis and noticed that they were not very successful, after being carried out for a number of years. We arrived at the conclusion that strategies which called for the teaching of agriculture or animal husbandry have not proven to be popular as a means of empowering ex-slave populations. Those kinds of undertakings seemed to have evoked aspects of past experience, which the Black race was seeking to forget. Moreover, the children, within one generation seemed to have internalized the experience of their parents as to be wary of toil associated with the land and of being once again entrapped in the commerce of animal or crop production. In addition, they were barred ownership of large acreages and farmsteads. So, of what use was farm training, or the knowledge of animal husbandry, if access to land was not forthcoming?

In 1852, in the center of the Black community we opened a new three-story building bearing the name, The Institute for Colored Youth, ICY, with a Liberal Arts curriculum taught by an all-black faculty. We had some resistance from parents about hiring White teachers. The school was in the vicinity of Sixth and Lombard Streets in Philadelphia. This time we took in both male and female students. It would be more than just a high school, being equipped with a library to which the community would have access. We hired Charles L. Reason as principal who was a liberal man with a passion for Science and Philosophy. We approved of his vision for the school and its purpose in the community. As an institution it provided a series of lectures on a variety of topics of which the community would be allowed to participate.

We were very excited about this new direction. The success of the school began to attract the attention of educators and planners. Many of them were White. On an average, we had a dozen and more visitors every week. Some of them were not well-wishers, but were anxious to endorse the Dred Scott decision handed down by the Supreme Court that Blacks were inferior and did not possess any rights.

Ebenezer Bassett succeeded Charles L. Reason, who took a job in New York. Mr. Bassett served for thirteen years before becoming Minister to Haiti and the Dominican Republic in 1856. Now we were faced with a dilemma. We began to search for a principal who could replace Mr. Bassett. ICY had become the pride of Philadelphia and the showpiece for Black education, and we hoped to maintain this standing. The problem of who should be chosen to succeed Mr. Bassett was soon resolved. We had two very qualified teachers on staff, Octavius V. Catto and Fanny Jackson Coppin.

At this juncture I am pleased to say we demonstrated a spirit which was the most forward-looking for the times. We hired a woman as Principal. Fanny Jackson Coppin was to become a pioneer in the field of higher education. She became the first woman to be appointed as head of an institution of higher learning in these colonies. Mr. Catto did not take it very well, proclaiming: "I will not work under a woman!" Fanny's solution was that moving forward she was willing to share the responsibility, with she, as principal for the girl school and he, for the boys. She valued his experience and advice. What a gal!

Not too long after I had taken up the position at Cheyney as director of Admissions, I had a surreal encounter with Fanny Jackson Coppin. I happened to be in Baltimore and paid a visit to Coppin State University, the small public institution named after her. In her honor, there is a beautiful bronze bust in the University library. I stood for a while looking at it and it was as though she had re-entered the land of the living. We had a silent conversation of the mind:

"I was born a slave in Washington DC, in 1837, because my mother was a slave. I don't know my father. My mother never talked about him. My aunt Sarah bought my freedom for $125. My grandfather had bought the freedom of his five other children except my mother."

"Why was that so?"

"On account of my being born out of wedlock, I suppose."

"You did not talk much about your mother in your book."

"I hardly knew her. Mostly I lived with my aunt Sarah. I owed so much to her. Do you know she worked for $6 a month and out of her meager wages she saved up that money?"

"She obviously had recognized something special in you, Ms. Fanny, that was worth the sacrifice."

"Yes, she did not really want me to go out and work as a servant, but I did not want to be a further burden on her, and the rest of my family."

"Was there anything in your childhood you especially remember?"

"I must have been about four or five years old, and I had this mark along the side of my leg. I asked Aunt Sarah about it. She said when I was

a child at my christening party, I was placed in a cot too close to the stove and the heat burned the side off my leg. Another time I was with my grandmother and a piece of coal from her pipe fell into my bosom and burned me. I still have the scar. My grandmother was probably losing her sight."

"I see you dedicated your book, <u>Reminiscences</u> to your aunt. How old were you when you gain your freedom?"

"Thirteen or fourteen, maybe. Soon after I left DC and went to live with another aunt in New Bedford, Mass. My aunt was able to get me my first job."

"Doing what?"

"As a servant to a family with whom I lived. I was allowed to go to school when I was not working which amounted to two days a week. I did not make much progress in my studies, so I went to Newport, Rhode Island instead, to live with another aunt through marriage."

"Why was that?"

"Well, there was a job with another family where the conditions were better."

"In what way?"

"Well Mr. Calvert was a great grandson of Lord Baltimore, the man who founded Maryland. His wife was a descendant of Mary Queen of Scots. The pay was better than my last job. I would have more free time to attend classes since they had no children. I first started at the Public Colored School where I could prepare for the entrance exam to enter the Rhode Island Normal School."

"When did you first know you wanted to teach?"

"While I was studying at the Rhode Island Normal School, there were teachers who encouraged me, both White and Black. I felt that I had a purpose to help my people and I owed it to my Aunt Sarah who had invested in me. I wanted to make something of myself."

"I understand that you played the piano."

"Yes, I was first introduced to it in DC, and while working for the Calverts, I continued to take music lessons every Wednesday."

"Are you aware that some folks today in the 21st century think of you as the myth breaker?"

Blushing, "No what myth did I undo?"

"Well, it is known that when you heard Senator John C. Calhoun declare that if there was one Black person around who could conjugate a verb in Greek, he would give up his belief that the Negro was inferior. Not only could you do it in Greek but also in Latin."

"Yes, that was the statement that kept me motivated to complete my degree. I refused to give up."

"On entering Oberlin, you were somewhat warned that the Gentlemen's Course of study you planned to pursue was very challenging and that women tended to shy away from the Greek, Latin and Math content. Why did you choose to go that route?"

"How could I not, I had a myth to undo. Right?"

"Yes, and you did it in style, Ms. Fanny. What was Oberlin like in those days?"

"It was a hotbed of activity before and during the Civil War. I graduated in 1869. It was the first college to openly accept Black students. About 5% of the school's population at the time I was there. I guess we were part of that 'Talented Tenth' Du Bois was referring to."

"I read somewhere that Charles Grandison Finney who was the President of Oberlin when you were a student was often heard to say that women were morally superior to men."

"President Finney was very encouraging about my plans after graduation, and I think he was the reason I was allowed to teach in the Preparatory school while still an undergraduate. These positions were generally given to white upperclassmen to teach. My students were White

and many of them were surprised upon entering the class that I was the teacher when they first entered the class."

"You started teaching ICY in 1865. What was the atmosphere like at that time?"

"I remember a conversation with Ebenezer D. Bassett that he and I had. He was reminiscing about the many visitors to the Institute to observe the students. There was this White researcher who had written a book about the inferiority of the Negro. He had heard about the success of the school and decided to pay a visit before finally sending off the manuscript to be published. He was accompanied by a friend who was a math teacher. This teacher wrote several problems on the board and asked for a volunteer. Jesse Glasgow volunteered. He solved each problem as fast as they were written down. Suffice it to say the book never was published. Jesse entered the University of Edinburgh in Scotland many years after leaving ICY."

"I must congratulate you on the magnanimous gesture of sharing the duties of the Principal of ICY with Octavius Catto after his little tantrum about refusing to work under a woman."

"He was too invaluable. I could not afford to lose him to another school. We were all devastated when he was killed. He had been shot on the day that Philadelphians went to the polls. His murderer was acquitted despite the eye-witness accounts."

"Sadly, gone but not forgotten. There was a peaceful protest of hundreds of people recently in front of his statute in City Hall by people of all races during a Black Lives Matter protest to call for an end to injustice."

"That is beautiful. Richard T. Greener was able to take on some of his responsibilities after he died."

"Yes, he was the very first person of color to have graduated from Harvard. I must share this with you. Some years ago, there was an old, derelict house outside of Chicago which was about to be demolished. A

member of the demolition crew found a trunk of papers and documents by Mr. Greener that must have been in the attic for decades. Harvard is interested in acquiring the collection."

"Wonderful! After leaving the Institute Mr. Greener studied law and was a professor at Howard. Oh yes, he was very active in the Republican Party and had several political assignments. He loved teaching at ICY."

"I always think of you as a change agent. By that I mean you always seemed to know the directions that were needed in terms of educating young people to meet current needs."

"Thank you I like that name! Change Agent. I'll tell you a story. One day I was on my way to school, and I noticed a building going up in the Black neighborhood and there were no black workers. I noticed all around me people of color were underrepresented in the Mechanical and Industrial trades. And I said to myself, I have to extend the curriculum. Plans were already underway to introduce a course in Teacher Training. So, it would take a lot of effort to convince the Quaker Managers to fund another program. But I got busy. First I needed to bring the idea of Industrial Education to the community."

"I imagine you had some resistance. But Ms. Fanny, knowing you as I do, you have pioneering blood in your veins. No one could stop you when you got going."

"There will always be resistance to new ideas. I visited literary societies, churches, organizations in Philadelphia, New York and Washington. I talked about the need for this type of training and its cost. I spoke about job opportunities for boys and girls and that the type of training we could offer would be available to the community."

"Did you have to cut back on Academics once the trade school was added?"

"No. The trades were mainly taught as a night program for people in the community working during the day. In the end we had collected

three thousand dollars through the pennies and dollar campaign which was matched by other large donations. Ten trades were introduced into a new building in 1879."

"You know Booker T Washington would have been a young man in the South then. I am sure he heard about you and ICY, and what you were doing. Maybe the idea for Tuskegee began with you Ms. Fanny."

"Well, I wouldn't take credit for that. Other people in the South were setting up programs like that. Tuskegee Institute did start out as a normal school which later became an Industrial Institute a few years later."

"I must tell you that your ideas for child-centered education were ahead of its time. They have been adopted by many school districts today in the 21ˢᵗ century."

"Really! I have always felt that as teachers our role should be more of a facilitator. I never agreed with stopping to correct a child while he or she was reading. It destroys the whole interest of what the lesson is about. I prefer to wait until the child was finished."

"Getting back into the sexism that you encountered as a professional woman and I must say that we women have made little headway in achieving an equal footing. I loved the way you handled that Presbyterian minister when you visited England."

"Well, first of all, sexism is a companion to patriarchy. They go hand in hand. And as for the minister he suggested while speaking to a group of women that they should never consider any ecclesiastical functions."

"Well, that certainly got you riled up, Ms. Fanny. How did you respond to that?"

"Well, the next day, I had to address the meeting and I raised the issue. That it was God's place alone to limit women's roles in the church. Furthermore, that even though we were created second, we had both a body and mind. It was true that God created fools but not all women were fools."

"I love that response. You retired in 1902, the same year ICY moved to the Cheyney Farm location on a 125-acre site."

"Yes. I was then 65 years old and not in the best of health. It was time to pass the baton into more able hands. The student body had outgrown the Lombard Street facility. The interest in the Normal School surpassed the classical curriculum in Greek and Latin. So, it was decided that moving forward ICY should concentrate on Teacher Training."

To this day, Cheyney University still focuses on Teacher education, in addition to awarding degrees in over thirty major fields of study. This incredible woman had shaped the pattern for the education of children of color for all of thirty-seven years as a teacher and school principal. She was constantly attuned to the educational needs of the Black community. It is safe to say that she blazed the trail for teacher training which was further developed by Cheyney University. Cheyney is, and has been, the first port of call for many a school district seeking to employ African American teachers.

When I was the Director of Admissions, I was able to reopen the Pittsburgh market with the help of two alumni- Booker Reeves and Sylvester Pace. The number of Pittsburgh students had fallen off tremendously when Mr. Reeves had retired from teaching in the Pittsburgh Public Schools. I paid a visit to his house during the first month of my tenure. He was no longer very mobile, but he had some great suggestions for recruiting students from Pittsburgh. For many years he had been an avid recruiter for his alma mater. On many occasions he would charter a bus paid out of his own pocket and would have Pittsburgh students make the five-hour trip to visit the campus. Sylvester Pace, a successful entrepreneur, who ran a College Access Program for students seeking remediation and guidance had been a valuable resource and pipeline to Cheyney while I was there. I mourn the passing of these two stalwarts who are gone but not forgotten.

Having worked at a predominantly White university before, as a recruiter of African American students, I can say in all honesty that there will forever be a need for this HBCU. I noticed that the angst and uneasiness that Black students experienced in and out of the classroom on White campuses, hardly reared its disabling head at Cheyney. Perhaps students felt that their intellectual abilities were less questioned. They seemed to speak up more in class. As an administrator, I was also able to teach a class in Third World Literature. It was the very same course I taught on the predominantly White campus. The difference then was that there were perhaps two or three students of color in the class who participated little during discussion. At Cheyney students did not have any reservation about talking about their experiences and that of their family. Their level of confidence was marked by an acceptance as well as by the encouragement of their classmates to share their experiences. Furthermore, they did not feel that their presence on campus was unwelcomed and begrudged.

The Student Ambassador program was the most authenticating voice during our open house. It became an integral part of the recruitment process. Students volunteered to call prospective students and to host them on campus. It was heartwarming to behold the degree to which students took ownership and pride in their school. Cheyney pride is steadfast and resolute. In the words of the Cheyney song, during which Cheyney calls to them, they kneel in supplication and proclaim: "All the honor and the glory, Alma Mater, shall be thine." Today when I meet graduates, there is such an abiding sense of loyalty, "with a deep and true devotion" to this school that gave them self-worth and an appreciation for their culture. It was a place that supplied the missing links to the history of the Black race. For so often they were told in their formative years that they were a people without a history.

My Cheyney years away from my home in Pittsburgh, and the separation I experienced from my husband were remarkable, in that I entered into a phase which was marked by a search for a deeper spiritual meaning to my life. While my days were filled with the concerns of students and the challenges of meeting recruitment goals, I felt lonely and isolated, for I was not part of a community. My life did not extend beyond the campus. At the end of each day, I returned to my tiny one room apartment. I knew and understood that my purpose was to use what knowledge of recruitment I had gathered while working under an astute and dedicated African American administrator, my first boss. I also had before me the essence of Richard Humphreys and Fanny Jackson Coppin as role models and the need to continue their work, and to this end I had come to accept this assignment as a form of 'ministry'.

While I was not overly pious. I believed in a divine Creator and, once in a while, I saw the workings of divinity in my life. I took to reading the Bible as well as the words of the Dalai Lama. I studied the lives of deeply religious men and women such as Mother Teresa and Dr. Albert Schweitzer, two people who had dedicated their life to a missionary cause. This period of my journey also was accompanied by a deeper understanding of the purpose of my life. To be sure, organized religion and the carnage in the wake of its proselyting mission, were problematic for me, even though my husband and I had joined the Methodist Church. I had many a conversation with my pastor, Dr J. LaVon Kincaid, to whom I am forever grateful for his timely responses to my questions seeking clarification of theological doctrine.

It was also a time in which I continued to mull over the nature of home and to consider that my roots in America had now become entrenched with the Cheyney experience. Now that I was part of the African American community, I felt that I had a responsibility to use my gifts in recompense. For I felt that an identification with a place one considers home and homeland must involve a willingness to share one's knowledge and skills.

Several years ago, after graduating from Clarion University, I was taken into the fold by the Dean of Admissions and had found purpose in working with students of color on that campus. That was the occasion when I was differentiated from among the many faceless foreigners existing outside of the body politic and be given a seat at the table of fellowship. I believed that I was called to Cheyney University for a purpose, and I was happy to have been allowed to make a contribution. During the six-year period I was there, we the staff, students, alumni, and faculty worked as one unifying force towards improving admissions. The result was that we were able to set a course towards an upward trend.

During those six years, I served as Director of Admissions, I was also delighted to witness the restoration of the historic quad, for it made it increasingly easier to promote the campus. When I left for Pittsburgh in June, 2007, I felt that I had completed my mission. There was a new President on board, with new ideas. The time had come to pass the baton, in the same way that Fanny Jackson Coppin had done a century before.

CHAPTER 27

In Search of Identity

"There is no gate, no lock, no bolt that you can set upon the freedom of my mind."

-Virginia Woolf

SOON AFTER LEAVING CHEYNEY, MY husband and I took a trip to England. I had not seen my sister in many years and so after my father's death, I had made a promise to myself to visit her. This trip was essential for another reason as well. I wanted to travel along the byways and highways of this land. I wanted to recapture the essence of a past era that spoke of Empire. Maybe a visit to the British Museum or the birthplace of the Bard, William Shakespeare would help me to develop a better understanding of the concept of Empire. This was the imperialistic authority that was so instrumental in setting the tone for my formative years. In those days, as children of Trinbago, we focused our gaze outward and across the sea. Then our look towards England as the Colonial Mother was all that we knew. I felt that being among 'Britishness' could assist my discovery of the essence of who I am.

I recalled the many occasions when I was young, we children of Trinbago would lift our voices and sing the British national anthem – God Save The Queen, with an intense pride and reverence. We would genuflect to the Union Jack. Did we children believe we were part of the Empire as we sang "Rule Britannia/Britannia Rules the Waves/ Britons, Never, Never, Never Shall be Slaves"? But we were descendants of slaves. So, from whence cometh this notion of belonging to the Empire? We worshipped at the shrine of British manners and nobility, so Princess Margaret's visit to Trinidad in the mid-nineties was a memorable event. My mother took us to Port of Spain to see her, as it was a momentous occasion. No one would dare to miss that event!

The whole island turned out to see the Princess. We lined the streets for miles hoping to catch a glance of her royal face as she was driven through the city. That day we travelled by bus. It was the first-time we natives ever saw a member of the royal family. It was a delightful occasion. We basked in the pomp and splendor of the nobility, the red carpet, the parade of the armed forces, the dignitaries and their wives with hats and gloves, the Governor, British at that time, decked out in the finest regalia appropriate to the occasion. The Princess was the representative of the Crown, Her Royal Highness, Queen Elizabeth II. A petite and confident woman, she moved gracefully among the waving natives sharing a word here and there. My young mind wondered about the trappings of royalty and whether they experienced pain as we poor folks did, or knew what hunger was.

As a child, I learned about loyalty to England from an early age, but soon I wondered about those accounts of the lives of children who lived in the Mother country who were portrayed in the books I read. When I would skim through the pictures in my Reading books, there was a feeling of distance, both in time and space. Time, in the sense that I was existing in an age long gone, sort of backward-looking, and in a place that the Almighty had forgotten. In my books, children like me were not represented in the stories of Jane and her playmates, who seemed to enjoy a lifestyle that was modern and stylish. They wore beautiful clothes, fashionable and dressy, even while at play. They lived in charming houses and had happy smiling faces. They appeared to be loved and sheltered.

As a youngster, I spent a great deal of time thinking about the Queen and her Empire. I wondered if our Colonial Mother did not consider us worthy of her affection. If that was true, why? We demonstrated love and respect for her, just as the children portrayed in our books. But blighted sucklings that we were, we hung unto her breast. I concluded, therefore that she did not love us. It was apparent that she was bent on enclosing us under the veil of servitude, according to my innocent thinking. As 'mother' and provider, she was lacking in maternal instincts. In my young mind the Queen appeared to be a self-serving ogre who declared ownership of our native talents and domestic resources, all to her advantage. Like a robber, she purloined all that was bestowed to us by the Creator, those natural resources and qualities necessary to improve and develop for generations to come. Our essence was reduced to serfdom with a grinding hostility, that cramped our vigor and deprived us of vitality. And then she declared us to be a race of people, to be slothful and dull.

As I grew older, these sentiments proved to be reinforcing, as they summoned up a unique pride in who I was. I believed that I had the option to prove them wrong and that I was responsible for my own development, and to make something of myself. Furthermore, I was constantly encouraged by some of my early teachers to strive for excellence. They reminded me about the common perception of the colonizer's view of the colonized and warned that by refusing to do my best was to feed into the stereotype. I became resolute. I was determined to rise to the occasion, for growing up under Colonialism,

I surmised, could be the hand that struck me down or raised me up. I would use this experience as one of elevation.

When I was a child of eight or nine, my parents knew a woman from Jamaica who worked for a prominent family on the island. This family lived in St. Clair, one of the wealthy areas on the island, generally populated by the nouveau riche and the representatives of the Crown. The head of the family was a Black man born in Trinidad and was one of the few, at that time, to have been granted a scholarship to study Medicine in England. As a surgeon, he was well respected and was married to a widow and mother of four. She was White, and British and chose to remain on the island after the death of her first husband. Her children were in boarding schools in England. Her diseased first husband had been a government employee sent down from England to bring culture and enlightenment to the natives. Occasionally, our Jamaican 'auntie' would have my sister and me spend a day with her, usually when the family was away. We slept in the servant's quarters which was a separate building from the house, low lying with a faint odor that reminded me of horses.

These visits were remarkable in the sense that at such an early age, I came to realize that there were Black people on the island who did not live on the brink of starvation and in a state of privation. I thought about their means of escape. My 'auntie' and her boss were of the same hue, but he stood at one end of the continuum and she the other. He was rich, and she was poor. What was responsible for the gulf? At that age, I thought the color and hue of the well-to-do was White and light.

A few years later at the age of thirteen or fourteen my father was a chauffeur to a Chinese dentist who invited my parents to celebrate the Chinese New Year with him and his family. His parents shared a house with him and his wife. My father took me along since I was the least self-conscious and the more sociable of my sisters. Again, I was amazed at the luxury and richness which surrounded the family - the resplendent tropical garden enclosing the house, the furnishings, the tapestry, and the modern appliances. On this occasion the color of wealth was yellow not White and light as I once believed. His parents were from the old country. They were drawn in from the Far East as indentured servants when slavery was abolished. They had owned a small dry goods shop, with living quarters at the back of which they eked out a home for their family. What accounted for this propensity to bridge the divide, and to break out from the constraints of the color bar?

Sometime between the age of twelve and sixteen I had become an avid reader. Two words were indelible on my mind. Upward mobility. I discovered the potency of these two words through a reading of English Literature. The theme of social mobility was everywhere to be found in the works of the masters throughout the centuries- Shakespeare, Dickens, Charlotte and Emily Bronte, D. H. Lawrence, Jane Austin. Their novels helped me to understand the potential to climb out of the confines of one social class into another higher and more wholesome one.

Whereas in England, several ways led to upward mobility, such as marriage or a sudden windfall from a distant relative, in Trinidad the path was narrow and torturous. The key towards advancement was through education, preferably university training in the professions such as medicine, dentistry, law, and finance. However, in Trinidad under colonialism, up until the middle twentieth century only a few secondary schools existed that offered a classical education. Furthermore, the opportunity to obtain a university education depended on winning an island scholarship as graduating seniors to attend a university abroad, since The University of the West Indies in Trinidad, as we know it today, did not exist, with access to graduating seniors. The English were unambiguous about their approach to education after emancipation. In Trinbago, it was not to create ladies and gentlemen, but gardeners, artisans, servants, and laborers.

Throughout the colonial period, the Crown begrudgingly held on to its principles of education for the natives. A few primary schools were built to focus on the trades and a couple of normal schools were created to train and mold a supply of tradesmen and servants to keep the plantation economy in motion. As the arbiter of knowledge, the Colonial Mother floundered like a rudderless ship at sea during a turbulent storm. Her unspoken motto: keep them ignorant and keep them contained. It informed the grand design by which she governed all her territories. Opening the floodgates of knowledge through the type of classical education she reserved for her own at the seat of the Empire and sparingly extending it to the colonies for the children of her administrators, was a dangerous feat with serious consequences. To allow each and every child access to a classical education in the colonies was to drive a nail in the coffin of colonialism. For wherever nationalism reared its militant head in Africa, India, or the Caribbean, it was always as the result of a learned few who dared to question the role of the Empire. India, 1857, during the early days of anti-colonialism is our witness. She summarily closed a number of schools and universities in India and Egypt, when nationalism threatened her position.

Britain's apology for colonialism was called manifest destiny, which was meant to bring freedom and liberty to the black, brown, and yellow races of the world to which she lay claim. According to her we were barbaric and ignorant. A hundred years of occupation, nevertheless, seemed to have plunged us into a deeper cavern of servitude. Notwithstanding, entire generations of people under her rule, such as my parents, could hardly read and write. Their role in life was no better than that of a serf to fuel her plantation economy.

While growing up during the closing years of colonialism, I acquired a sort of down-to-earth approach to the experience, that was somewhat practical. My belief was that the leaders of the newly independent state of Trinbago should distinguish from among the habitual customs and beliefs of the colonizer, those practices that were worth keeping, and those that should be jettisoned. For what use is the rhetoric of blame?

As an example, the British classical education system, which once was available only to a few, was kept and tweaked for future generations. It was the basis upon which a curriculum more suited to the West Indian student was built. It was a good system that taught me how to write, read and think critically. I often wondered what would have been the fate of my parents' generation if they were privy to it. We had seven years of high school and were taught the sciences, foreign languages, mathematics, and the arts. A few years after Independence this system of education produced a group of black, brown, and yellow professionals, men and women, though mostly men, educated in Trinidad and Britain. They were returning to champion the cause of nation-building. The presence of these professionals was what the colonizer feared and sought to avoid at all costs. The myth of the dull and ignorant native was under attack, for in a short space of time, we were able to emerge from under the umbrella of the master. In the words of the Black American female poet and essayist, Audre Lorde, we were able to use "the master's tools" to "dismantle the master's house."

When the British left, in 1962 at the dawn of Independence, our country was poverty-stricken. There was no infrastructure, no reserves, and no industry to which we could lay claim. For years, the British search in the Americas for the mythical El Dorado, the city of gold, was useless. As luck would have it, around the turn of the century, the faithful land of the hummingbird, Trinidad, cracked her seams to reveal an asset of a different hue, not the yellow color she once dreamt of, but black - black gold, crude oil, which in some places was flowing freely to the surface. Britain promptly claimed this resource. Although our forefathers made attempts to wrestle the resource from her hands in a move towards self-governance, she promptly rebuffed us, claiming we were not ready to rule ourselves. We were still too illogical, lacking intelligence and jejune. But were we? She had not reckoned on John Jacob Thomas. As a result of his brilliance, he managed to have gained admittance to one of the few secondary schools opened to her sons and daughters.

Froudacity! A word coined by John Jacob himself. He was a natural linguist, conversant in French and English, and was the son of ex-slaves. One day in 1888, so the story goes, the English writer and Oxford trained James Anthony Froude, visited Trinidad for a few days. On returning home to England, he published a travelogue in which he made some startling claims about the ineptitude of the Black race in Trinidad to be able to govern themselves. That was the impetus for John Jacob Thomas to write a book in which he presented a series of counterarguments to the writing of James Anthony Froude. Thomas claimed that it was pure audacity on the part of Froude to appear to be an expert on the Black race, the lifestyle, the character, and aspirations of a people whom he had observed from afar. "Froudacity!" he explained to a captive audience while giving a public lecture on the subject "was a common colonial trait, and one which was to be found throughout the literature, the travelogues and novels of the times". I thought of Conrad and Kipling. Remember _The Heart of Darkness_?

John Jacob Thomas was born in 1841. He studied the Creole grammar, which was then spoken by the majority of workers and their families. Having served as schoolmaster and civil servant in 1888 he travelled to England to publish his two books, _Froudacity_ and _Creole_

Grammar. Soon after he contracted pneumonia and died at the age of 49. By then he had left a startling legacy for generations of colonized peoples to examine and take notice. I oftentimes wondered....

How many such as he
whose brilliance glowed
With thumbs down
was denied
A fair shake, an even break
Due to his ebony hue?
His race for generations
Had yielded forth
A sapient world of enlightenment,
In Egypt in the East
In Benin in the West
That drew Napoleon and Alexander the Great
And all who sought insight and refinement.
Froudacity! The effrontery
The sass and arrogance,
Be gone!

I discovered the works of John Jacob Thomas during my freshman year at the University of the West Indies. I marveled at his clarity and command of the English language. He was conversant in French, English and the patois spoken by the ex-slaves having grown up on the plantation. His book on creole grammar was an attempt to position the language in a more favorable light, showing that it had a structure and syntax. During the nineteen and early twentieth centuries every attempt was made to eradicate the patois as spoken by the ex-slaves and their descendants. English was to be the only acceptable language taught in the newly established ward schools and used in the courts of law. By the time the British left in 1962, the French patois was totally lost.

My paternal great-grandmother spoke the French patois. She was born to African slaves in the early period following emancipation. I remembered hearing her speak it. I also knew that she did not understand English very well. My grandmother and my father, on the other hand, spoke both English and the French patois. Ironically, as with many things lost to us today, there is an attempt to revive it. However, very few people alive today in Trinidad have ever heard it spoken. The tragedy is that the loss of a language could also mean the loss of an oral account of a people's history.

I enjoy reading the Greek tragedies by Sophocles whose account of the fated Oedipus and his progeny is thought provoking. I marvel at the strength and resilience of Antigone, the daughter of Oedipus. In the play, she faced death as she made attempts to bury her favorite brother Polynices, whose body was left to the crows because he was considered a traitor. I am amazed that I could still find value in reading the two epic poems of Homer in his account of the Trojan war in the *Iliad* and its aftermath in the *Odyssey*. Much of the Greek literary tradition originated in the oral accounts passed down from one generation to another in Greece, thousands of years ago, before they were written down. But more relevant is the impact the Greek oral tradition has had on Western literary tradition of which the West Indian cannon has emerged. I shudder to think of what would have been the fate of Literature had the Greek oral accounts been suppressed. I often wonder whether in extinguishing the patois, we destroyed valuable oral histories. Were we depriving the present generations of a folk hero like Antigone, who may have stood up for her people as they were transported through the Middle Passage? This is mere speculation, but we would never know.

CHAPTER 28

Lessons from the Metropole

"The worst thing that colonialism did was to cloud our view of the past."

-Barack Obama

A VISIT TO SHAKESPEARE'S BIRTHPLACE in Warwickshire, England, brought back memories of when my class first read his last play *The Tempest*. Our discussion had centered around Prospero as the benevolent and altruistic Robinson Crusoe-like settler of an island with one inhabitant, Caliban. Prospero was the Duke of Milan, who was neglectful of his responsibilities, as he pursued magic and his books, and whose brother Antonio wrested the dukedom from him. He was then placed on a rudderless ship to roam the seas along with his three-year old daughter Miranda.

Upon being washed up on an island during a storm, Prospero immediately embarked on a conquering mission to bring culture and language to the only inhabitant of the island – Caliban, who was the son of a witch. According to Shakespeare Caliban was Black, grotesque, and wild. Caliban quickly mastered the language but bemoaned the loss of his own native tongue and folklore. He became increasingly resistant, accusing Prospero of usurping all that he once held dear. He longed to revert to the time before Prospero claimed his island, culture, and language – in essence, his birthright.

During my class reading and discussion, I recalled that we could find no fault with Prospero to whom we ascribed high moral values, culture, and enlightenment. We despised Caliban for his fault-finding and abhorred his surliness and defiance. He was viewed as being coarse and uncultured, forever to remain a savage. Our socialization into British ways dictated that there was no hope of refinement other than through Western culture and the English language. We had no history, our folkways were dull and boorish, and our native patois lacked structure and legitimacy. For as long as I can remember, we sought respectability through mastering the English language and the ways of the Colonizer.

Years later a second reading of _The Tempest_, for my class in Postcolonial Literature, imparted an entirely different perspective. I now saw myself as a descendant of Caliban - as Caliban's daughter. A fresh reading of the play changed my perspective such that Caliban appeared to be a representative of Fanon's _Wretched of the Earth_, from whom was wrested the rightful ownership of tribal and indigenous lands. I no longer viewed Prospero as the benevolent master determined to bring culture and enlightenment to the ignorant natives. Instead, I interpreted his actions as that of a pilferer and destroyer of native cultures and languages.

Growing up colonial has left an indelible mark. I cannot escape the compass of the Empire, no matter how hard I try. Colonialism has imposed constructs on how I should think and behave, as well as the language I use to communicate. I am forever on my guard to ensure subject-verb agreement, to refrain from ending my sentences with a preposition and to avoid the vernacular at all costs. When possible, I tend to shy away from any aberration in syntax which immediately could type me as someone of a lower-class status, thus lacking respectability. I am constantly vigilant about what constitutes proper and socially acceptable behavior, to evade being perceived as coarse and unrefined, lacking in grace. Hence, for those of us who grew up in a British colony, the colonial yardstick as the measure of our decency and self-worth is somewhat difficult to escape.

I admire the brave who seek to fight back against the empire. "How do you 'decolonize' the mind?" I once asked my professor in post-colonial Literature. I admire African writers in poetry and novelists such as Ngugi wa Thiong'o who are writing in their native tongue rather than a hegemonic language such as French or English. I recalled that my first attempt to write a story about Papa Bois, the guardian of the animals and other African/Trinbagonian folk-lore characters such as La Diabless, the devil woman with one cloven hoof, and Soucouyant a vampire-like character. My writing attempts were doomed to failure. While growing up, I often heard oral ac-counts of these characters by the old people in the village. I wrote sev-eral drafts in English which I eventually abandoned. They never felt right, the dialogue felt out of place, contrived and false. As a result, I understood why Ngugi felt that the African experience could not al-ways be expressed in English. Once again, I thought of Shakespeare's plays written in Old English. I believe that modern translations do not do justice to the flow and rhythm of the dialogue as spoken dur-ing the time in which they were written. Perhaps more importantly, contemporary renditions of the original plays lose something of the authenticity of the period, not the least of which are the original cus-toms, mores, and settings of the times.

I mourn the loss of the language of my great-grandmothers. Such loss of a language invariably results in the deprivation of stories and myths, especially accounts of early settlement with the indigenous peoples of Trinbago. My great-great-grandparents must have heard the Creation myths as told by the Arawaks and Caribs, who were the first occupants of the land. As succeeding generations of the peoples of Trinbago, we do not have a creation myth such as those of other indigenous peoples. A Creation myth often tells the story of how a people usually came to belong to their ancestral home. The creation myth we now claim as our own is not unique to us. It is the myth of millions of Christians. We are not even sure where this Eden of Adam and Eve is located.

The Caribs and the Arawak were the indigenous peoples who once lived on these lands. They were exterminated because of the oc-cupation of waves and waves of conquerors over the centuries. The indigenous people possessed a Creation myth passed down from one generation to the next, which explained how they happened to be rightful owners of these lands. They had an invested interest in pro-tecting and safeguarding the environment, the land, and the waters of the rivers, which sustained their lives. We, the new peoples were brought here by a race bent on exploiting these lands. We the new peoples from Africa, India and parts of Europe had no connection to this place through a Creation myth which informed us about how to live with our environment. Instead, we the new peoples have inher-ited the ethos of the exploitation of nature. Our depleted coral reefs, as well as the extinction of some of the native animal species due to overhunting are examples of the exploitation of our island habitat.

The trip to the metropole raised an important question for me, one that I have often revisited. I question the significance of Creation myths for displaced peoples. I wonder if it were possible that I could have a genuine attachment to a place that I could call homeland even though my ancestors were not in possession of a

Creation myth like that of the indigenous peoples, that originally located them to Trinidad. In addition, since my ancestors were neither Carib nor Arawak, could I call Trinbago my homeland? If I could not call Trinbago my ancestral home, then what accounts for this strong feeling of nationalism towards Trinbago which I feel? It blossomed with the advent of the nation state and continues to grow. Does this feeling equate in some way with an adherence to a new variant of the Creation myth, which was reconfigured at Independence, that now extends to all people who are born and are buried in Trinidad?

Still for expatriates such as myself, who have left the land of their birth to inhabit another place, does the Creation myth of the new and distant land apply to me even though I was not born there? Are there other ways I can claim another country as homeland other than through a creation myth? I am thinking about myself and my sister Janet who left home on our own accord because of marriage, education and training, and job opportunities for a more comfortable life? Maybe the idea of a creation myth is no longer relevant in the modern era in which we live, due to the incidence of widespread movements of people in this global environment. To many the notion of home as a geographical place appears to be declining in relevance in the twenty-first century.

My sister, the epitome of a twenty-first century world traveler, is married to a British engineer and has lived in many countries. More recently, she has settled in England for half of the year and the other half in Miami, to escape the brutal English winter months. We talked about the meaning of home, in terms of which country she considers best suited to the idea, as a place where she feels she can relax and was welcomed.

"I feel like flotsam and jetsam sometimes. I seem not to have roots anywhere. I have lived in six different countries."

"What about Trinidad? Surely you have roots there?" I asked.

"True I did not leave until I was a grown woman. And it is where our parents are buried.

But it is a different place from what I knew. I am thinking of the experience of our great grandmother Julia when she returned to Martinique."

"We still have family there, a sister, her children and some distant cousins."

"Yes, but the feeling of the place is not the same. Everyone seems so young." She responded.

"What about here in England, the home of your husband?"

"Living here in the southwestern part of England, where I don't see many people of color, I have little opportunity to be part of a community with people such as myself. I have one or two white friends but when I am here, I tend to keep to myself."

"I imagine it's the same thing in Miami. Most of the people in the gated community where you live are transient such as yourself."

"Yes. They are snowbirds from Canada and other areas where it gets cold in the winter. Again, I am a transient. A greeting here and there but no concrete friendships."

"For half of the year, you live within the confines of the old empire here in England. How do you feel about the past?" I enquired.

"Sad. I look around and wonder what they did with all the wealth which was taken from colonial territories. There does not seem to be much on display to account for it."

"Oh, it was all spent in acquiring the trappings of war – which as you know are expendable. The empire had to give up her territories by the end of World War 11. She was virtually hurting for money. In the eighteenth and nineteenth centuries, England stole art treasures from India and Africa. When I visited the British Museum, I saw a replica of the largest diamond on display that was taken from India. Do you know that in the British museum most of the collection is from the colonies?"

"It should be called The British Colonial Museum. What was not taken and housed for display was suppressed." she explained.

"Absolutely. I was amazed to have discovered that there were Trinidadian authors who had published novels from as early as the mid-1850s. These were from Black and Mulatto writers. Where were those books when we were growing up? *Rupert Gray* by Stephen Cobham would have been a great read since its portrayal of a Black man who was an accountant and knowledgeable in the Sciences would have been a great role model."

"Exposure of those works never would have worked. You know that Gem. The protagonist, Rupert Gray married a white girl. Black/white sex was taboo in those days."

"Only for the colonized, Janet. White/Black sex for the colonizer and miscegenation was a different matter."

"That was the theme of _Emmanuel Appadocca_ another early Trinidadian novel we did not have access to. The author was a Mulatto, Maxwell Phillip." She replied.

"You know Janet, the empire has left such an indelible mark on my mind. Sometimes, I feel it tugging so much against my sensibilities, that I am not sure of my Caribbean-ness"

"I see what you mean. You and I married the empire." She stated with a smile.

"True. My first marriage was to a so-called Trinidad White. You see the problem was that growing up even though we were told by our teachers that as Black and Indian children we were not inferior, there was a sense that moral and cultural superiority and respectability were to be found only within the empire."

"Yes, you could be punished for speaking in the patois in those days. But there have been some advantages to the British presence."

"I agree. For one thing, there were improvements such as the railway system, telecommunication, plumbing and road construction. These advances, however, were not widespread but tended to be concentrated in the pockets where the colonizer lived. But within a generation after independence the framework was there to be built upon and extended." I pointed out.

"We also had the library which provided access to the outside world, although most of the literary works were by British and American writers. I think there were two newspapers from the middle nineteenth century for those who could read."

"British Literature has been very crucial in helping me to understand the imperial mind and eyes. I value it immensely and now living in America, I am on a new quest to discover the American psyche."

"I think that living in America has been good to you Gem."

"In many ways, it has. I have found my soulmate."

"So now you understand that home is where your soulmate lives?"

"Yes, I am beginning to think it can be in more than one place."

"For me it should not be confined to place. Given what we are witnessing with respect to refugees and displaced people, immigration and exile, I think a search for home has got to be a journey inward of a place in the heart where the love and acceptance of family and close friends reside." She explained.

"I understand. If my family and I as well as my close friends, were to be place on a deserted island, it would be home because it would be where my heart is?"

"I would say yes, regardless of place," was her response.

After my visit with my sister in England, I had a better understanding of my identity and of what constitutes homeland.

Furthermore, I am older and wiser now and more forgiving of my colonial upbringing. In addition to my 'Caribbean-ness', I now think there is much to gain by an exposure to different cultures. Would I be the person I am if I had not been introduced to the music of composers such as Beethoven or jazz greats such as John Coltrane? It is difficult to assess how the literature of other cultures have shaped my sensibility. Would I be the same person had I not read the novels of Thomas Hardy, Charles Dickens, Jane Austin and the plays of Shakespeare and the works of Toni Morrison, and James Baldwin? Opportunities to read the poetry of Walt Whitman, the tragedies of Sophocles and the epic stories of Homer, even the literary criticism of the Palestinian-American Edward Said, who I have labored intensely to understand, have all contributed towards shaping my world view. I am learning to live with what the empire has made of me, because I have made peace with her portrayal of my ancestors as being a sable race, dull and indolent. I forgive her because I know otherwise.

CHAPTER 29

Living in the Time of the Pandemic

"We must keep an endless watch on ourselves lest in a careless moment we breathe in someone's face and fasten the infection on him."

-Albert Camus

AMERICA, THE LAND OF THE free and home of the brave! While I live under the American flag, I have come to accept this place as my adopted homeland to which I owe allegiance. My husband was born here, and while it is not my native homeland, the land where my parents are buried, it is a place where I have also found meaning and self-worth. Living in these times of the pandemic has stirred my sense of moral obligation. I felt that the 'stay-at-home' orders were a personal plea that was directed towards me. I understood it to be a plea to do my part to defend the homeland while it is under attack from the pestilence, and to wear the mask of protection in defiance of the onslaught of the virus. Now I had to put aside personal interest for the safety of the wider community.

I was no stranger to a call to action that was imbued with responsibility to help others. While growing up, I sought to encourage the people of my village of El Dorado to consider modern medicine rather than the traditional ways of the 'Obeahman.' Another call to action occurred during my time as a recruiter in the African American community. I had to encourage young men and women to pursue higher education. This call-to-action had brought on such a heightened feeling of responsibility and self-worth, that I felt I had become an 'evangelist' for education and the surrogate 'Ma,' who on campus, was determined to ensure that my recruits persisted and graduate. In return, I was welcomed into their homes and was treated as though I was a favored member of the family. Out of these experiences arose a conviction that perhaps one's home was not always connected with one's birthplace. The same acceptance and appreciation could arise through concern for the success and welfare of others who are not blood relatives. Concern for the welfare of my adopted community was the reason why I accepted the position at Cheyney University. At that time, it was expedient to temporarily relocate to eastern Pennsylvania to fulfill a promise I had made to my mentor, the Dean. Now in these times of the pandemic, I felt that while most of us are not trained to be first responders, we all have a responsibility to ensure that we are not the cause of infecting another person.

My search for further meaning in these times of the pandemic led me to a rereading of Albert Camus' *The Plague*. I was particularly drawn to his observations about how effective a pandemic can be in calling on personal responsibility to family, home, and country, to ensure that we are not responsible for infecting anyone. At first the statistics relating to COVID-19 were misleading and somewhat innocuous, as to indicate that it was no different from the regular annual flu season and that it would soon die down. Also, we have had pandemics in the 20th and 21st centuries such as the Aids virus, Spanish Flu, the Asian Flu, and the Hong Kong Flu. None of these, however, has been as pervasively threatening to our health and well-being and as easily transmissible as COVID-19.

It is ironic that never before have I spent so much time at home, with an occasional visit to the supermarket being one of the few times when I make contact with the outside world. As I reflect on my life, it seemed that in the past, I was always 'on the go.' Now the pandemic is bent on reshaping my present existence. Similarly, my husband who was often away, either gigging or consulting, has had to reconfigure a way to practice his craft from home, and has managed to use the technology to continue working.

Home as a place where family and friends reside has a strong emotional content attached to it. For many who no longer live at home, there is an urge to be with family and friends, especially during the holidays. It is a time when customs die hard, and when millions of people in these times of the pandemic, risk the danger of contracting the virus and spreading it, while trying to get home to family. These are the occasions when an increase in the numbers infected seems to stem the tide of efforts to deal with the virus. Very often I am besieged by a certain image that readily comes to my mind - of Sisyphus rolling that enormous boulder uphill to reach the top, only to have it come tumbling down again to the bottom.

The 'stay-at-home orders' to protect us from the virus have come to highlight that aspect of home as sanctuary and a safe haven - that it may be the only place where one is most likely to escape the contagion. The 'stay-at-home orders' are also important in ensuring the welfare of the wider community. However, at times the task of safeguarding the community seems to be in direct conflict with the need to be with family and friends. Not too far from where I live is a municipal park with several undercover pavilions. The pandemic has not discouraged those who have come to celebrate birthdays, graduations, weddings, reunions, christenings, and gatherings. No one wears a mask at these events. We are by nature social beings, who thrive on connection, and for whom isolation can be experienced as a form of imprisonment. As I hurry along to escape these gatherings, I am overcome by a feeling of déjà vu. I seem to be reliving the past when there was no virus and things were normal.

While I miss the past when I could go dancing, attend a concert, or visit my family in Trinidad, or even have them visit me, I realize that there is a danger when 'stay-at-home' could come to feel like being in exile. The freedom to come and go, that we once took for granted, would have to be curtailed to safeguard ourselves and others. To this end, I am constantly in search to find ways of altering my dull routine and realigning priorities and not wasting time. I now seek ways of living in the present and not pining for the past. These days my husband and I have taken the opportunity to make a series of day trips to visit many historical sites and to return to the town where we were married.

Sometimes I see no break in the cloud. There seems to be no receding of the high-water mark in this rise of the pandemic. I feel like flotsam floating on a sea of anonymity. Wearing a mask to keep myself safe and others from infection, I am less recognizable. When I meet friends, I am not expected to say more than the usual pleasantries. I make less eye contact. The pandemic has confined us to the mere nominal aspect of day to day living such as preparing meals, attending to bodily functions, domesticity, rest, and exercise, with little to no time for the social component of daily living. I miss the society of friends and family. This year marks the first time in twenty years I will not celebrate the holidays with my family from Trinidad.

Living with the pandemic is akin to having the sword of Damocles hoisted above one's head. It is no less than a prolonged state of isolation, the result of which brings out the best or worst in people. The sign at the entrance to my neighborhood grocery states that there would be no entry without a mask. Recently while shopping, I happened to witness a woman in her mid-fifties who walked in without a mask. Stopped by the security guard, she tried to force her way in, without success and after several minutes, left in a huff, while creating a scene and using a string of expletives towards a man trying to do his job.

While I understand the frustration and difficulties of the times in which we now live, I try not to judge people's actions. In Camus' novel _The Plague_, Father Paneloux delivers a sermon in which he claims that God was punishing the citizens of Oran for their sins. Suffice it to say that the plague did not spare him and eventually he succumbed to it. I struggle to avoid taking this virus personally, and I question why we should be experiencing a pandemic at this time. I try to refrain from ascribing sentient qualities to the virus. While I know the virus cannot hate or does not have the ability to think rationally, I cannot help but question the environmental benefits we have witnessed such as the improvement to the ozone layer that has occurred within the past year.

I know it will peter out sometime in the near future. But when should we expect this to happen? It is also referred to as the novel coronavirus or (nCoV). Hopefully, the common experience of fear and the likelihood of infection will bring nations closer together and by the time of its exit, we would have a new understanding of the systemic inequalities of the world. Hopefully we would become more acutely aware of the environment and how it impacts humanity's very survival. It is my hope that the peoples of the world will come to embrace the beauty in many cultures, in plurality and that an understanding that a striving towards homogeneity among races will only lead to ethnic cleansing, genocide and extermination, of one race of people by another.

I wear a mask as I traverse the paths that meander in and around the pavilions and ball fields in the park nearby. A game is underway, and the path is blocked by spectators sitting on camp chairs remarkably close to each other. I must divert my steps to go around them to keep a safe distance. In the distance I hear the sudden firing of the guns on the rifle range. And I think of the men and women on the front lines who are the heroes in this war of fighting a highly contagious virus, while some of us insist on carrying on as though Covid-19 is a figment of the imagination.

When I think of those frontline heroes, I have moments of catharsis and hope. I believe once again that my adopted homeland will win the battle. I put aside my selfish feelings of boredom and isolation and try to harness the power of conviction in my fellow man that they too will see the importance in putting aside individual happiness in favor of moral obligation to the larger group. This is what our homeland requires of us in times of danger. As we struggle with possible illness and perhaps even death, self-interest only seems to aggravate the situation. Staying at home is a call for solidarity in purpose, for we are better able to bear the weight of our fear when it is shared.

CHAPTER 30

A Place to Lay My Head

"Homelessness is a nationality now."

- Margaret Atwood

FINDING HOME AFTER A LONG sentimental journey, to determine whether it was possible to have the same sense of loyalty to more than one place, was also a quest of an existential nature to gain some insight into the person I am and my purpose for living. While the pandemic keeps me captive, it has also provided moments of solitude to reflect on being among family and friends here in America. That awareness is so compelling that I am convinced that I am home. I discovered that my sense of being home coincided with those periods when I was most involved with the community of young people, and with the event of my marriage when I was treated to a red-carpet welcome into the Stemley family. On both of these occasions, I felt I received the key to the city and that I could enter unannounced, for I was home. Still, can I say in all certainty then that I had found a place where I could rest my head in peace? As a foreigner, was it possible to be at home in more than one country? Could I become an adopted child of the land where I now reside? Furthermore, do I have anything to say to my great grandmother Julia about finding a home in a country that is not the place of my birth?

Many years ago, when I left Trinidad to take up studies in the US, it was not merely to acquire better prospects for employment upon my return. A kind of thirst also drove me to experience a landscape beyond the limits of the horizon of my island home. I was familiar with the cultural milieu and literature of the Caribbean. So, I sought to experience the back yards and spaces of James Baldwin, Toni Morrison, Gwendolyn Brooks, and the landscape of Walt Whitman's _Leaves of Grass_. I was ripe for change and sought to extend the boundaries of my island, of which I was most familiar, and out of which I had never traveled. In addition, I was fearful of descending into a sort of provincialism or narrow-mindedness and of being accused of a lack of sophistication. I thought an experience of a different cultural milieu was necessary to broaden my perspective.

However, once I had settled into this new place, this land at the epicenter of modernization, I began to harness the power of my humble ways of knowing, to share with young boys and girls a possible means to escape the cycle of poverty through education. To my delight, my message gained some traction and resonated in the minds some. It was at this time that I seemed to have found purpose and commitment to a community of people who were appreciative of what I was doing and who were eager to open their hearts and minds to what I had to share. I felt that I had found a place in the Black community and that I was among family, for I was a person of color, I shared a similar history, and I knew their pain.

As I reflect on those early days when I struggled to come to terms with my decision not to return to my homeland in Trinidad, feeling that I had 'sold my birthright for a mess of pottage', I had one consolation. The work I had undertaken was not motivated out of self-interest but instead, with a willingness to share the lessons of my early upbringing, and later the knowledge I had gained under my mentor, the Dean. Furthermore, I reflected upon the many Trinidadian authors, artists, entertainers, and academicians living abroad and the acclaim and spotlight they had brought to Trinidad and Tobago. I did not feel that any one of them had felt they had abandoned their homeland. I then considered myself somewhat of a goodwill ambassador, whereby I lay to rest those troubling, persistent feelings that I had sold my birthright. After all, Trinidad was the only country where I could obtain a birth certificate.

Did my marriage to an American, and my acceptance into his family conflict with my love for my family back home? No. In fact, now I am welcomed in two countries where I would not be denied shelter and a place to lay my head. My intercultural marriage has been the occasion whereby I can lay down roots in America, in addition to my roots in Trinidad. I feel that I am on firm ground. As the years have gone by, I have frequently returned to Trinidad to keep abreast of the changes that have taken place within the cultural scene. Now, that Trinidad is not too far behind the cutting edge of technology, with the assistance of the internet, I am increasingly able to track daily the political and social climate. As a result, I have a more realistic understanding of my native land.

This new way of perceiving reality, and this foray into self-discovery was crucial to my understanding of how I once thought of my early upbringing and my homeland. I felt I needed a better perspective on how I viewed reality and that by going forward, I needed a clearer insight into my past if I were to handle those demons that were barriers to growth and enlightenment. I chose to tap into the wisdom of the early philosophers. Plato's *Allegory of the Cave* provided me with some insight. It is a story told twenty-five hundred years ago by Plato in his work, _The Republic_. _The Allegory_ appeared in Book V11 and was narrated by a character in the likeness of his teacher and philosopher Socrates, whom Plato loved. Socrates is talking to his young friend Glaucon, about how people perceive reality. He tells him to imagine a cave with a long entrance which is opened to the outside. There are people in the cave who have been chained to their seats from childhood. They are unable to move their heads sideways or up and down. Nor can they walk around in the cave, so they have never been on the outside. They can only see what is in front of them which is a wall in the cave.

Light comes to them from behind, from a fire which is burning close to the entrance. Between the fire and the prisoners is an elevated walkway where people move along in either direction with loads on their heads of plants, animals, goods, and utensils. Their shadows are reflected on the wall in front of the prisoners. They see these shadows and think they are real. But what they saw were only representations of reality.

One day a prisoner escapes and climbs out of the cave. At first, he is blinded by the fire and the light of the sun outside, and experiences tremendous discomfort and pain. He looks at the fire and the people moving about and is confused. What does this all mean? He cannot believe that what he saw in the cave all those years were mere shadows. Now that he is outside of the cave and can look around and talk to people, he realizes that his cave experiences were but an illusion.

Like the cave dweller, I considered that I once inhabited a cave of illusion, during the visit to Trinidad with my husband when I acted as guide to my island paradise. At that time, my only option was to climb out of the cave into the sunlight. Gradually, I saw through the dysfunctional nature of my upbringing marked by a stark absence of memorabilia in the house where I grew up. Where was the evidence that all was well with my family? Why were there no pictures of family hanging on the walls? Where were the pictures of my grandparents, or certificates of achievement, graduation, wedding pictures, albums that captured those delightful moments of youthful pranks? The house where I grew up was so devoid of memories as to suggest a determination to erase the past.

My foray into self-discovery while outside of the 'cave of illusion' was also the opportunity when I was able to critically examine my internalized experience of socialization under Colonialism. It was an acceptance of the British aesthetic standard which served only to subvert our cultural values and disparage our language. We lived with the notion that respectability was only to be found in Britishness - in the English language, the Protestant religion, allegiance to the crown, their standard of beauty, British manners and customs, formalities, and etiquette. Only recently did I discover the writings of Black and Mulatto authors who lived under the Colonial government and whose works were not available to the general reading public in Trinidad at that time. English Literature was what was promoted. Most of my early days were lived out in conflict with feelings of inferiority due to teachings of the Colonial masters. To a certain extent, I continue to grapple with the Empire, having found it difficult to completely dispense with feelings of anger associated with the exploitation of our resources.

Regarding Trinbago, I was still in the 'cave of illusion' during my early visits back home. The way I experienced my homeland, especially on visits to escape the stress of modern day living in America was like that of a visitor. At that point, I intended to luxuriate in the sunshine instead of using Plato's allegorical 'sun' to examine the conditions of what was taking place in the modern society of Trinbago. Even then I chose to lay aside the concerns of Trinbagonians and to avoid all signs of disquiet in my Eden. However, I soon realized that if I were to continue accepting Trinbago as my homeland I had to face up to reality and dispense with the notion of Trinbago as paradise. I had to come to terms with Trinbago as a modern society in the 21st century with all the attending evils associated with drugs, unemployment, and poverty.

While finding a home in America, I have been mindful about neither re-entering the 'cave of illusion' nor inhabiting the American ethos – that the good life corresponds to chasing the almighty dollar. I have also needed to disavow the notion that these United States are a perfect union, or that the American dream has meaning for all. The important thing is to know what the reality is in order not to be blindsided.

In the end, as long as reality is forever before me, America is where I choose to live when I am not in Trinidad. It has become my adopted homeland as well for the reason that in America, I can continue to pursue self-mastery at the same time while living a meaningful life. I value opportunities for intellectual pursuits and exploration, which I associate with living a good life. There is an aspect of the vastness of this land that has strengthened my courage to venture out to undertake new pursuits. For example, my resolve to work at Cheyney University in the face of opposition from my friends meant that I had to live away from my home in Pittsburgh for a period of six years. Courage has become very liberating and has offered up a kind of freedom. Here in America, I can explore more fully the many ways to work with young people to advance their dreams. I also enjoy harmonious and respectful relationships with people from different ethnic backgrounds who have become an integral part of my experience.

While I often think of home in terms of geography, such as when I say that home for me is Pittsburgh or El Dorado and homeland is Trinidad or America, there is an aspect of home that is not confined solely to place or country, rather to the mind and heart. Recently my sister was separated from her family in Trinidad for eight months, due to the closure of the borders in Trinidad during the pandemic. She often claimed: "my home is in my heart where I value the love and relationship with my family. It is not defined by place." My sister Janet who has lived in many countries, also claims this to be her experience of home as being in the heart. Perhaps this is the way I sometimes experience home when I am not in Trinidad. Maybe it has something to do with a common experience or aspects of what Carl Jung considered to be part of the "collective unconscious?"

I can say that my journey to a distant land where I have come to experience what the notion of home means to me, was primarily guided by love. Firstly, the love for the community of young people with whom I was able to find meaning and purpose. Secondly, and most importantly, the support and love of my husband who has become my co-pilot on this journey who wants to ensure that I am at home in the land of his birth. His guidance oftentimes is directed towards the psychic dimension of my experience. He reminds me to be aware that the American ethos which is centered on prosperity and success can take a heavy toll on one's physical and psychological health. He observed how my left brain has tended to govern most of my waking hours. He is aware of my mortal fear of failure in all that I do. I seem to be too driven to determine my vocation and to ensure that I was always on track to carry it out. He is all too familiar with my difficulty in sitting still and not engaging in meaningful tasks. He worries that I am too logical and analytical.

My husband, being a right-brain thinker has sought to point out to me the meaning of harmony and balance, and has inspired me to go out on a limb of creativity beyond the confines of my left brain. This coincided with the time when I was encouraged to play the flute, at an age when I never would have entertained the thought. Or when I took it upon myself to create a garden. I filled the entire bed with flowers of all heights, shapes, and color in no specific order. However, when I considered the final effect there seemed to be chaos and a lack of symmetry. My husband suggested that I should consider the function and beauty of space, which in music was an important feature along with dynamics that provides variation in loudness and phrasing. I imagine that music without space and dynamics would not be pleasant to listen to. For space gives the impression of being able to breathe and has an overall effect of freedom and freshness. As I thought of it, I appreciated that the concept of space could be paired with a desire for moderation in all that I do. Starting with just a few plants I was able to create a feeling of depth and symmetry by the way I allowed adequate space between each plant and its position in the bed. I learned that the same approach could be carried over to how I structured my waking hours.

Finally, while I continue to have one foot in the land of my birth and another in the land of my adult life where I have found love, I am reminded of the occurrence in nature referred to as the homing instinct. As the years go by, I still experience a strong pull towards the land of my birth. This call to return home is most powerful around events such as my birthday and the anniversary of my parents' passing. Perhaps it has something to do with the pull of the placenta buried in the land of my birth that once gave me nourishment. Maybe it is a call from the spirits of my parents and grandparents.

Epilogue

THIS MEMOIR HAS BEEN A quest to determine whether the émigré can experience home in a country other than that of his/her homeland. It took on significance many years ago while I was growing up in Trinidad. It was a time when I often spoke to my great grandmother Julia about the meaning of home and homeland. I was deeply affected by the angst and misgiving she felt returning to Martinique, the land of her birth. She left for Trinidad on that fated day in 1902 for Trinidad when Mt. Pele erupted. Upon her return almost half a century later, she could not recognize the place. Trinidad, where she finally settled and was married with children, became home to the extent that she had raised a family there and it was the land of her husband but not where her parents were buried. Still, within her, there was this yearning to return to a place with which she could not identify. The question of whether home could be in more than one place, or no place at all, continued to be a question in her mind until her passing. Many years ago, I left Trinidad to pursue studies in America with all intentions of returning, but my life took a different course.

If my great-grandmother were still alive, I would share with her that I am constantly and deeply aware of how she felt on her return to Martinique. As a result of this awareness, I try to return home more frequently to avoid the feelings of loss and disconnection she once felt. Furthermore, I would tell her that I try to keep up with the daily happenings using technology. Even though I observe changes in the social and natural landscape when I return to Trinidad, the changes are more tolerable. I would share with her that I have found it possible to find home in more than one country and to accept a foreign land as my adopted homeland. I can do this through a feeling of commitment and self-worth. Through love and personal growth, I have discovered a path to a more meaningful life. Being married, I am now part of an extended family with roots in Trinidad and America. Yet despite all of these insights and experiences, underneath it all, there is still a persistent beckoning to the land of my birth. Even though I have found peace, love, and contentment in two very distinct homelands, there will always be present the yearning to return home as a result of the powerful force called the homing instinct:

That innate sense
whereby the pigeon harks back to its roost
and where the salmon defies all odds
to return to spawn.
What of this homing instinct?
Does it ever melt away like the fallen snow,
or dissipates like an echo in the night?
Does it fade like the stars at dawn
Or the dewdrops on a blade of grass?
Maybe it is like the ebb and flow of the riptide
That never ceases
Or the mystery of the setting sun
That rises again, without fail.